Two week loan

Please return on or before the last
date stamped below.
Charges are made for late return.

General Editor: M. Rolf Olsen

TAVISTOCK LIBRARY OF SOCIAL WORK PRACTICE

Managing Social Work

Managing Social Work

TERRY BAMFORD

TAVISTOCK PUBLICATIONS
London and New York

First published in 1982 by
Tavistock Publications Ltd
11 New Fetter Lane, London EC4P 4EE
Published in the USA by
Tavistock Publications
in association with Methuen, Inc.
733 Third Avenue, New York, NY 10017

Printed in Great Britain by
Richard Clay (The Chaucer Press) Ltd
Bungay, Suffolk

British Library Cataloguing in Publication Data

Bamford, Terry
Managing social work. – (Tavistock library of social
work practice)
1. Social work administration – Great Britain
I. Title
361.3′068   HV245
ISBN 0-422-77960-1
ISBN 0-422-77970-9 Pbk

Library of Congress Cataloging in Publication Data

Bamford, Terry.
Managing social work.
(Tavistock library of social work practice)
Bibliography: p.
Includes indexes.
1. Social work administration.   I. Title.
II. Series.
HV41.B2556   1983   361′.0068   82-14143
ISBN 0-422-77960-1
ISBN 0-422-77970-9 (pbk.)

Contents

General editor's foreword

Tavistock Library of Social Work Practice is a new series of books primarily written for practitioners and students of social work and the personal social services, but also for those who work in the allied fields of health, education, and other public services. The series represents the collaborative effort of social work academics, practitioners, and managers. In addition to considering the theoretical and philosophical debate surrounding the topics under consideration, the texts are firmly rooted in practice issues and the problems associated with the organization of the services. Therefore the series will be of particular value to undergraduate and post-graduate students of social work and social administration.

The series was prompted by the growth and increasing importance of the social services in our society. Until recently there has been a general approbation of social work, reflected in a benedictory increase in manpower and resources, which has led to an unprecedented expansion of the personal social services, a proliferation of the statutory duties placed upon them, and major reorganization. The result has been the emergence of a profession faced with the immense responsibilities of promoting individual and social betterment, and bearing a primary responsibility to advocate on behalf of individuals and groups who do not always fulfil or respect normal social expectations of behaviour. In spite of the growth in services these tasks are often carried out with inadequate resources, an uncertain knowledge base, and as yet unresolved difficulties associated with the reorganization of the personal social services in 1970. In recent years these difficulties have been compounded by a level of criticism unprecedented since the Poor Law. The anti-social work critique has fostered some improbable alliances between groups of social administrators, sociologists, doctors, and the media, united in their belief that social work has failed in its general obligation to 'provide services to the people', and in its particular duty to socialize the delinquent, restrain parents who abuse their children, prevent old people from dying alone, and provide a satisfactory level of community care for the sick, the chronically handicapped, and the mentally disabled.

These developments highlight three major issues that deserve particular attention. First, is the need to construct a methodology for analysing social and personal situations and prescribing action; second, is the necessity to apply techniques that measure the performance of the individual worker and the profession as a whole in meeting stated objectives; third, and outstanding, is the requirement to develop a knowledge base against which the needs of clients are understood and decisions about their care are taken. Overall, the volumes in this series make explicit and clarify these issues; contribute to the search for the distinctive knowledge base of social work; increase our understanding of the aetiology and care of personal, familial, and social problems; describe and explore new techniques and practice skills; aim to raise our commitment towards low status groups which suffer public, political, and professional neglect; and promote the enactment of comprehensive and socially just policies. Above all, these volumes aim to promote an understanding which interprets the needs of individuals, groups, and communities in terms of the synthesis between inner needs and the social realities that impinge upon them, and which aspire to develop informed and skilled practice.

M. ROLF OLSEN
Birmingham University
1982

To Margaret, Andrew,
and Sarah

Acknowledgements

This book would not have been written without the assistance of many friends and colleagues. I am particularly grateful to Rolf Olsen who first encouraged me to undertake a work on this subject and then advised, guided, and supported me throughout its preparation.

To all my colleagues in Harrow Social Services Department I owe a special debt for the ready interchange of ideas and the stimulus of discussion, which is in some small measure reflected in what I have written. My particular thanks go to Keith Bilton, whose clarity of thought has helped to resolve some of my confused ideas.

I have quoted liberally from *Social Service Teams: The Practitioner's View*, edited by Phyllida Parsloe and Olive Stevenson. It helped me to identify the critical issues facing social work managers. At a time when the value of management courses is sometimes questioned, I gratefully record appreciation of the help received from two short courses provided by the Institute of Local Government Studies, University of Birmingham and by Brunel University respectively. I thank too Chris Brown, John Cypher, Anthea Hey, and Eric Morrell for their help on particular issues discussed in the text. The typing of the book has been undertaken by Pam Jackson, Litsa Mina, and Isobel Shrimpton, to whom I express my gratitude.

The case examples used are drawn from different social work settings and from several local authorities. Throughout I have used the masculine form to describe social workers and managers. This is to avoid the stylistic inelegance of he/she and for no other reason.

Finally, I thank Margaret for her encouragement, and Andrew and Sarah for their forbearance, as Dad did his 500 words each evening.

1

Management matters

Management and Social Work are uneasy bedfellows. The application of management principles and techniques to social work agencies is still relatively young. The utility and relevance of management has been increasingly questioned by social workers struggling to find their professional identity, but finding management disabling rather than enabling. The Barclay Report has discussed the relationship between organizational structures and social work practice. The role of management in social work is thus at the forefront of current debate about social work and its future direction.

It is surprising therefore to find how little has been written about management in social work in contrast to the rich and ever-growing literature about social work practice. This book aims to direct attention to management, and to develop the argument that skilled and sensitive management can have an immense influence on the quality of current practice and the evolution of practice as services develop.

The impact of local government

The integration of professional and administrative hierarchies in social work agencies tends to be taken for granted. The major public sector social services – local authority social services departments and the probation service (in Scotland social work departments) – have a unified structure with a social worker serving as Chief Officer. The advantages of such structures were thought at the time of their establishment to be the strong social work input at all levels of managerial systems, and thus the creation of an administrative support structure responsive to individual needs and circumstances rather than a conventional bureaucratic response geared to precedent and long-established procedures.

In other European countries, this integrated structure is regarded with envy. There is immense potential for conflict in structures which divide professionals from administrative hierarchies. Why then has integration failed to achieve the goodwill and support of social workers? First and foremost it has to be recognized that a great sense of distance separates social workers from the Chief Officers. In most structures at least four grades are interposed between Director and social worker. The process of filtering information inevitable in any hierarchical structure thus has the effect of divorcing Chief Officers from the day-to-day reality of practice. Second, the reaction of senior management to outside criticism from successive child care inquiries, from the Birch Report (1976), and from the press has been essentially bureaucratic. It has been a local government response in terms of tightening managerial systems and controls rather than a social work response in terms of promoting good practice. As in any antithesis, there is an element of oversimplification in this polarization yet there is an essential truth in the description. Third, the wide salary differentials between local authority Chief Officers and the newly qualified members of the social work profession militate against the development of a shared professional identity.

The challenge posed to management is in large measure a challenge posed to contemporary concepts of local authority accountability. It is variously expressed as a criticism of local government itself as a focus for social work practice, as a criticism of the style of management imposed on social work agencies by virtue of their base in local government, and as a criticism of the organizational structures which have been adopted within a local government context. But while these issues have to be discussed in relation to local government, it has also to be recognized that similar tensions have been evident within the probation and after-care service, where the aspirations and objectives of Chief Probation Officers have not always been supported by main grade officers. After looking at the specific social services trends which have an impact on management–labour relations, it will therefore be necessary to look at the impact of broader social trends which also have an impact in this area.

Local government has been the base for personal welfare services since the early years of the century. When the reorganization of services was under consideration by the Seebohm Committee in 1968, the Committee excluded any consideration of locating social services outside the ambit of local government as beyond its terms of reference. In Northern Ireland, however, a different structure prevails with social services and health services administered by local boards. Similar proposals have been canvassed for mainland Britain from time to time. Apart from the advantage of unified service provision, it is argued that boards of this kind funded by central government would produce a more comprehensive and uniform pattern of service. At present there are acute differences in *per capita* spending in social services authorities, with the most generous spending over five times as much for each individual as does the lowest-spending local authority. Central allocation of resources also means that services enjoy some degree of protection against the vagaries of shifts in political control, which tend to be more extreme at local level than at national. Thus in recent years, both the National Health Service and the probation service have seen slow but steady growth while the expenditure pattern of local authorities has shifted on a year-to-year basis.

But the major argument deployed against local government is not the financial vicissitudes to which agencies are subject, but the expectations which managers have to satisfy in local authorities. The basic expectation is that the organizational structure will be based on hierarchical principles. The reforming legislation of the post-war Labour Government imposed extensive new duties on local authorities. The Children Act 1948 required local authorities to appoint a Children's Committee and a Children's Officer. The clear line of accountability was that of the Chief Officer to the Committee in whose name he acted. As a consequence the involvement of supervisory and managerial staff in decision-making was much greater than in a service such as the probation service with a highly developed tradition of individual personal accountability. This contrast is well illustrated by Section 2 of the 1969 Children and Young Persons Act. This empowers courts to make a supervision order placing a child 'under the supervision of a *local authority* designated by the order or of a *probation officer*'.

This upward pull of decision-making has had a pernicious impact on the structures adopted in social services departments by limiting the powers of the individual practitioner. At its most ludicrous, this finds expression in bureaucratic fantasies that all letters must go to and from the Director of Social Services or the Area Officer. But it is most prevalent in the way that decisions about admission to residential care, or cash payments to prevent the necessity for reception into care, are taken by senior managers rather than basic grade social workers. Thus whereas most professionals in local government – lawyers, accountants, architects, engineers – enjoy high status, the social worker is at the bottom of a managerial hierarchy, and whereas other local government professionals enjoy recognition for advanced practice, in social services departments recognition in salary and status has gone to managerial posts not to skilled practice. The effect has been subtly to devalue the contribution to the service of those in regular contact with clients.

Hierarchical structures are not without virtues. They give clarity about lines of accountability. They give authority to those at the pinnacle of the structure. They are common to many organizations, and thus readily understood. They are the conventional model in local government. Yet they inevitably create the sense of distance between top and bottom referred to earlier, and in departments where channels of communication are poorly developed that distance can soon become alienation.

Growth in responsibilities

The problems of senior management have been exacerbated by the major shift in the span of responsibilities throughout the personal social services. The creation of social services departments meant that many managers, whose previous experience was limited to social work decision-making, found themselves responsible for extensive day care, domiciliary, and residential services. The acquisition of new managerial responsibilities has not been peculiar to social services departments. The extension of hostel provision, the development of day training centres, and the mushroom growth of community service orders have presented Chief Probation Officers with new and unfamiliar responsibilities. Similarly, long-established voluntary organizations like Dr Barnardo's and the Church of England Children's Society have reorientated their activities from their historical base in residential care to innovative community-based projects.

Managers have thus been coping with responsibilities of which they had no previous experience.

The changes required from Directors of Social Services were even more far-reaching. Not only were they required to grapple with the broad spread of responsibilities within their own service area, but also to play a vital role in the emerging concept of corporate management. The structure of local government, which had remained unchanged for decades, came under critical scrutiny (Mallaby Report 1967; Maud Report 1969; Bains Report 1972). The Bains Report in particular advocated a break with the traditional pattern of effectively self-contained local authority departments and its replacement by a corporate structure headed by a Chief Executive outside the departmental pattern. Usually this led to a smaller group of Chief Officers supporting the Chief Executive in a senior management group and the Director of Social Services was a key member of this group.

This afforded new opportunities for social work thinking to influence the evolution of education, housing, and planning policies at top management level – policies of critical importance in terms of social welfare. Unlike their colleagues in Scotland, on whom Section 12 of the Social Work (Scotland) Act (1968) had laid the explicit duty 'to promote the welfare of the community', Directors in England and Wales were unprepared for these wider responsibilities. Social planning as a subject of study is still in its infancy, and Directors were forced to rely on native wit as much as professional knowledge in their input to corporate management. Thinking in macro-terms is difficult for social workers trained in a model of individual casework. Today's social workers have a better grounding. The unitary model directs attention to structural factors and the impact of social policy as well as to relationship problems, thus helping social workers to bring together the micro and macro-levels of intervention.

Not only was the training of many social workers who were promoted to managerial positions inadequate but also they lacked sufficient experience of practice fully to integrate that training. Between 1971 and 1974 the numbers of social workers increased by over 50 per cent with a concomitant increase in senior staff. Qualified staff were still in scarce supply. Promotion thus came very rapidly. A study in Southampton carried out by Neill and colleagues in 1972 (Neill *et al.* 1973) found that half the fieldworkers planned to change their job within two years. The increased volume of work, the greater span of responsibility, and the inexperience of subordinate staff created a defensiveness in managers which found expression in bureaucratic controls.

The economic recession and limited resources have stifled the creativity and individualized decision-making which were seen as the essential social work contribution to the new departments. Hey has described the outcome as 'bigger and better welfare departments. As such they owe rather more to a parentage traceable through public assistance, although hopefully suitably humanised to reflect current values and standards, than they do to the more professionalised and recent developments in social work' (Hey 1982: 17).

This comment raises the issue of the appropriate relationship between social work and the provision of direct services – domiciliary, day care, and residential care. The view prevalent in the years immediately following reorganization was that of social work as the dominant method influencing all sectors of the department with social workers acting as the key decision-takers over access to resources. That view came under increasing challenge with the evolution of the Certificate in Social Service, with the development in a number of local authorities of social service officers who have a primary responsibility for clients whose need is for practical provision, and with the contention that psycho-social assessment had little relevance to practical problems like the payment of fuel bills to avert disconnection. The appropriate link between social work and service delivery is still under discussion, but the issue underlies any consideration of organizational structures.

Common to all structures has been the preoccupation of service managers with area offices in the wake of Seebohm's recommendations. This has had two detrimental effects. First, area offices have rarely been local enough to meet the spirit of the Seebohm Report (1968) in terms of being a readily accessible focus for neighbourhood activities. The report itself, with its assumption that such offices could serve a population as large as 50,000 to 100,000, is blameworthy in this regard. The current interest in patchwork is in part the desire to achieve the intentions of the Seebohm Report while limiting the role of its chosen instrument, area offices, which have proved almost as remote and forbidding as the civic fortresses which formerly housed 'the welfare'. Second, the potential for collaboration with other agencies – social security, schools, GPs, day centres, voluntary organizations – has been impaired by the concentration of fieldwork resources in the area office rather than developing the role of 'outposted' workers. Thus for wholly understandable reasons area offices have increasingly become the bases for large groups of social workers.

What is being described then is a complex interlocking set of reasons for the failure of social services and social work departments to achieve what had been anticipated, and in particular their failure to produce job satisfaction for social workers. The shared professional values which had been anticipated as a result of social work's predominance in the management structure were not reflected in structures and working methods. That kinship of interest is helped by relatively small units. The probation service, where Chief Probation Officers often have less than a hundred officers, has a greater sense of unity than do social services departments.

Management has become increasingly identified by its staff with the policies pursued by elected members. Exercising budgetary control is seen as a covert way of making cuts. Redeployment of resources and rationalization of services are regarded as managerial euphemisms for reductions in services. Attempts to define objectives are criticized as restricting individuality and flexibility. A polarization of attitudes has taken place, with the interests of management and staff being seen as radically different. And as in most such polarizations in an industrial context, stereotypes develop. Managers are seen by social workers as the passive uncaring agents of councillors, and social workers are seen by management as unrealistic, woolly-minded prima donnas.

The gulf between managers and practitioners was observed by several writers (Glastonbury 1975; Bamford 1978; Brenton 1978), and in 1978 concern was sufficiently widespread for overwhelming support to be given to a resolution at the Annual General Meeting of the British Association of Social Workers. This declared that the present organizational structure of local authorities social services departments was harmful to the practice of social work, and urged detailed consideration to alternative structures more compatible with the nature of social work. The report of the working party established to undertake the detailed study was published in 1982 (BASW 1982). Predictably, it offered no clear-cut solutions. Issues of such complexity do not lend themselves to ready prescriptions of how structures can be modified. There is no consensus within social work about the causation of the problems, and even less agreement about possible remedies. The significance of the report may not be in terms of identifying solutions, but in keeping before elected representatives, managers, and practitioners an awareness of the tensions inherent in present structures.

Some of the models canvassed in the BASW (1982) report are considered in the final chapter. But there are dangers in yielding to the seductive notion that organizational change is the most effective way of improving the quality of management. Local government as a whole – and social services departments in particular – are prone to the fallacy that reorganization solves managerial problems notwithstanding abundant evidence to the contrary. The fault, dear reader, is not in our structures but in ourselves. This book therefore will not contain radical new proposals for patterns of organization which could transform the quality of social work provision. What it aims to consider are the skills required by managers, and how they can be developed and utilized within the constraints of a social work agency.

It is important that managerial skills should be improved if progress is to be made in securing better co-ordination of provision, better planning, and a better quality of service to the clients. Only when those problems which have stemmed from confusion about the nature of managerial responsibility have been resolved will it be possible to alter the structures and systems within which social work is practised. The chapters which follow look first at the changing environment which confronts social work managers, go on to consider various aspects of managerial responsibility, including the interrelationship with organizational structures, and conclude with an examination of the demands likely to be made of social work managers in the future.

2

Seebohm and after

The post-war social services were organized to meet specific problems at specific times – children in need of care, mentally disordered people in need of hospital treatment, the elderly seeking residential care. They were geared to meet symptoms rather than to look at the needs of the family and social circumstances in an effort to prevent break-down. The separate departments dealing with specific symptoms impaired effective co-ordination. As early as 1956, the Ingleby Com-mittee was set up to review services to juvenile courts and reported that 'the long-term solution will be in a reorganisation of the various services concerned with the family and their coordination into a unified family service', although the report went on to warn of the formidable difficulties in achieving this (Ingleby Report 1960:19).

The Ingleby Report recommended the establishment of family advice centres to offer information, advice, and diagnosis to families. It stressed the importance of adequate arrangements to ensure publicity and access for services – attitudes to be reflected nearly a decade later in the report of the Seebohm Committee. The Labour Party Study Group report (Longford Report 1964) and its successor White Paper *The Child, the Family and the Young Offender* (Home Office 1965) recommended the abolition of juvenile courts and their replace-ment by a structure of family courts. While the concept of family courts foundered on the opposition of the magistracy, the proposal further stimulated discussion of the need for a family service and created a climate in which the establishment of a committee to review the structure of personal social services was a logical step.

The Seebohm Committee was set up in 1965 'to review the organisation and responsibilities of the local authority personal social services in England and Wales, and to consider what changes are desirable to secure an effective family service'. In its report (Seebohm Report 1968) the Committee identified six major areas of weakness in the structure of services: inadequacies in the volume of provision, with services falling short of meeting identified needs; inadequacies in the range of provision, with neglected areas falling between the identified separate spheres of responsibility; inadequacies in the quality of provision, with insufficient staff, time, and training militating against standards; poor co-ordination between services which dealt only with a particular age group or a specific class of problem and failed to deal with the needs of the whole family; difficulties in access because of confusion about the pattern of services and divergent responsibilities; and insufficient adaptability in responding to new needs.

The Seebohm Report had no doubt about the model favoured for the 'new local authority department providing a community based and family orientated service, which will be available to all'. It sought to establish a large unified department, not only in order to reduce the fragmentation and duplication of existing services but also to create a powerful focus for resources. The report offered two reasons for hoping that a unified department would secure a larger budget. 'First, within local councils a committee responsible for the whole range of the personal social services would rank as a major committee. Secondly, and more generally, the greater simplicity and accessibility of a unified department is likely to expose many needs which have hitherto gone unrecognised or unmet' (Seebohm Report 1968: para. 47). That perception was accurate, but the expansion of a managerial hierarchy was to run parallel with the increase in resources.

The Seebohm Report did not consider any alternative structure to the hierarchical model found throughout local government, nor did it explore the implications for managerial control of the decentralized area structure which it advocated. In the tumultuous years following the Local Authority Social Services Act, 1970, the lack of guidance in the report led to the adoption of some confused and complicated administrative structures which subsequently had to be unscrambled. Despite the retention by Sir Keith Joseph, then Secretary of State for Social Services, of veto powers over the appointment of Directors, only rarely were appointments offered to candidates without relevant experience in social work. The backgrounds of those appointed were diverse – voluntary organizations, the probation service, the inspectorate, and universities as well as those already serving local government. The Seebohm Implementation Action Group fought a number of battles with recalcitrant councillors to ensure the supremacy of the social work profession in relation to these key posts, but the victories were pyrrhic in the sense that these struggles absorbed the energies of social work's activists while crucial decisions were being taken about the staffing and organization of departments.

The rapid expansion of social services between 1971 and 1974 led to the creation of relatively highly paid supervisory and managerial posts, which were filled by the most experienced and skilled practitioners. Promotion was rapid, and staff turnover became a major preoccupation in departments. For a profession whose training laid emphasis on consistency and continuity in relationships with clients, the conflict was acute. The National Children's Bureau study (Page and Clark 1977) gives a perspective on this from children in care. 'My brother and I have had more social workers than I can remember. They'd see us once and then disappear for six months, then we'd have a new one. And it's been going on all the time I've been in the home. They've been leaving or they've been going ill. And if that's happening all the time, I don't see how they can help you'.

Career grade

The British Association of Social Workers responded to this depressing pattern by establishing a working party on a career grade, which reported in 1975. That report starkly exposed the gap between professional expectations and local authority practice.

> 'The social worker has only limited accountability for his work – a principle which is sharply at variance with the normal precepts of a profession, of the practitioner accepting individual responsibility for his practice . . . the main factor is confusion about the professional identity of the social worker – is he primarily a social worker, or a local government officer?'   (BASW 1975: 283)

The report advocated a clear distinction between professional practice and administration, with equal reward and value being accorded to skilled practitioners as to those in management roles. Several local authorities devised schemes giving some recognition to senior practitioners, but the concept of a career grade received a major boost with endorsement by the DHSS Working Party on Manpower and Training for the Social Services (Birch Report 1976).

The working party skirted delicately round the issues of professional freedom at the core of the career grade argument, and concentrated on the need for a separate career structure for experienced workers in order to improve standards of practice. It saw the retention of experienced staff in direct contact with clients as critical to any overall improvement, for only thus could expertise be developed, alternative methods of service delivery tested, and knowledge of client groups or the needs of the area be progressively accumulated.

The attainment of a career grade at that time foundered on an incomes policy which allowed no scope for substantial upgradings and on the deep-rooted hostility of NALGO. Like most trade unions, NALGO believes that the level of pay for a particular post should be based on the 'rate for the job', not the individual abilities of the post-holder. A career grade explicitly based on individual merit was therefore unpopular with the trade union, which was suspicious that management would manipulate any such scheme to favour staff who did not 'rock the boat'. Hope of achieving a career grade died with the social worker strikes in 1978 and 1979.

These were the result of attempts in inner London boroughs to secure local agreements for a regrading of social workers in pursuance of official NALGO policy to abandon the national prescription of salaries. Individual local authorities resisted the pressure although an offer was made at one stage by the Greater London Whitley Council, seeking a London-wide settlement. Industrial action, and eventually strike action, was taken in those boroughs – Islington, Tower Hamlets, and Southwark – with militant and well-organized NALGO branches, and that action spread like a rash across the country with eventually as many as fourteen local authorities with social workers on strike.

The dispute was a curious one. Ostensibly it was not about pay. The issue was the right to negotiate locally. It was supported by NALGO, which paid generous strike pay, running down its strike fund by £2 million pounds in the process. Yet, except in Tower Hamlets, no other group of NALGO members took action in support of the social workers. Opinion within the social work profession was sharply divided with BASW failing to give a clear lead. The morality of taking action which would harm clients was much debated. The national leadership of NALGO vacillated in its attitude with a growing divide between the official and unofficial leadership. The strikes finally ended with an uneasy compromise providing for local negotiations within a national framework of three levels amidst cries of 'sell-out' from some activists.

The three-level profession which emerged from the settlement may be seen by some as a career grade. Yet the immense variations in the application of the national framework, ranging from areas where progression to level three is automatic two years after qualification to those where a limited quota of level three posts is enforced, have militated against the use of the scheme to reward good practice. Some authorities have sought to use the differential levels, allied to a system of staff appraisal, to reflect both the degree of difficulty in allocated cases and the degree of skill possessed by the worker. The categorizations adopted represent an uneasy mix of job evaluation terminology and concepts borrowed from the DHSS Report on Manpower and Training (Birch Report 1976).   *Levels 1-3. SW*

Level one was for those workers who:

> 'under close and regular supervision are expected to manage a caseload which may include all client groups and all but the more vulnerable individuals or those with complex problems. Such social workers are not expected to make decisions affecting the liberty of clients or in relation to place of safety orders.'

Level two workers:

> 'with supervision and advice are expected to manage a caseload which may include the more vulnerable clients or those with complex problems and may be expected to accept responsibility for action in relation to the liberty or safety of clients in emergency situations. They may be expected to concentrate on specific areas of work where such concentration arises primarily from organisational needs and to supervise trainees or social workers.'

Level three workers:

> 'with access to advice and within normal arrangements for account-

ability are expected to accept full responsibility for managing a caseload which will include the more vulnerable clients or those with particularly complex problems in situations where personal liberty or safety is at stake. Such officers are expected to contribute to the development of other social workers. They may be expected to concentrate on specific areas of work requiring more developed skills. They may be expected to contribute to the development of new forms of service.'

This settlement offered considerable scope for conflict between management and staff, conflict over the way in which the national framework was applied locally, over the anomalies between different local authorities, and over the impact of the levels on particular individuals. By increasing managerial power over grading, the settlement yielded the principle of a rate for the job which had led NALGO to oppose the career grade. The settlement was followed by increases for managerial grades so the aim of achieving parity of salary and status between practitioners and managers remained as remote after the strikes as before.

Nevertheless in terms of cash, the local agreements that followed could be argued as a justification for the strikes, for substantial increases were often achieved. The true cost of the strikes was to be paid later, however, in terms of lost credibility with public and politicians. The apocalyptic horrors prophesied by the strikers were not realized. No children died who might have been saved. No unsupervised old person died lonely and neglected. Like the firemen's dispute, the absence of social workers failed to exact the toll of death that some had feared. Yet if the prophecy of deaths can be put down to rhetorical excesses, the evidence of other forms of harm is scanty. Those who suffered were those already at the bottom of the pile in society – the powerless, the young, and the deprived. The costs of children remaining in residential care longer than necessary, of delinquents sent away because no social enquiry report was available, and of the silent suffering of an old person waiting for Part III are difficult to measure. The Social Work Service report on the impact of the strike in Tower Hamlets provides several illustrations of these private griefs, and concludes that the strike did seriously weaken the community supports available to vulnerable families (Howard and Briers 1979).

The press reaction to the dispute was often violent. The *Daily Telegraph* under the heading 'Unnoticed Absence' questioned whether social workers were necessary – 'Many tasks they perform ought to be done by the individual concerned, or by his neighbours and relatives, or by voluntary agencies – or, sometimes, by no one at all.' Lynda Lee Potter in the *Daily Mail* wrote, 'this long strike has surely proved that we can afford to curb the service, to pare it down and to ensure that we help only the needy.'

The strikes came at an unfortunate time when public expenditure restraints were imposing great pressures on social services departmental budgets. The change in the economic climate greatly increased the potential for conflict. The halcyon days of double-figure annual growth rates of the early seventies were suddenly halted. The Labour Government in 1974–75 made huge reductions in public expenditure. Many cherished plans for development of services had to be pigeonholed. The rapidity of expansion in the early years of the decade had created what Walt Rostow termed in a different context 'the revolution of rising expectations' – expectations stimulated by compassionate legislation, by the community orientation of area offices, and by the greater public awareness of social services provision. While resources could be controlled by central and local government, the expectations once stimulated could no longer be suppressed. The tension between community demand and available resources was to become acute. Beyond the political truism that need is infinite and resources finite, social services management had to find ways first of defining need, then of rationing limited resources to ensure that those most in need benefited from services. Priorities became the watchword of management and resulted in the adoption of various forms of priority scales to determine the allocation of time.

The experience of social services compressed into a few years the trend away from the concept of universality. The insurance principle at the heart of the proposals in the Beveridge Report (1942) has been whittled away by the growth of discretionary payments for specialized groups in need. Similarly the original concept of social services departments promoting the welfare of the whole community is now being challenged by a more limited view of a department supplementing the work of the voluntary sector.

In a speech to the Women's Royal Voluntary Service in January 1981, Mrs Thatcher spelt out this role: 'The volunteer movement is at the heart of all our social welfare provision. The statutory services can support the supporters and ease the pressure on volunteers with professional help and advice' (*Community Care*, 29 January 1981). Mrs Thatcher's perception constitutes a striking contrast to the judgement of the Seebohm Report that 'the day when voluntary organisations could act as vehicles for upper and middle class philanthropy appropriate to the social structure of Victorian Britain is now past' (Seebohm Report 1968: para. 496). While the report was enthusiastic in its endorsement of the value of volunteers, and the stimulus to statutory provision from lively, critical voluntary organizations, it in no way envisaged the limited role sketched out for social services departments by Mrs Thatcher. The current political enthusiasm for patchwork seems to owe much to a similar attitude, seeing statutory services in an enabling role rather than as directly service-giving. That notion is a chimera. There is no effective alternative to statutory provision for many – possibly the majority – of clients, whose needs for assistance are such in both volume and complexity that networks of volunteers are ill equipped to cope. The limitations and the possibilities of patchwork are considered further in Chapter 6.

The initial campaigns against the cuts were in reality protests against the abandonment of growth. No redundancies were contemplated in 1974–75, but the end to growth imposed severe strains within departments as managers sought to redeploy resources. The severity of reductions in capital expenditure, which stood by 1977 at a third of the level in 1974, meant that the focus of activity was perforce switched from bricks and mortar to community-based services, an emphasis broadly welcomed by professional bodies. Any attempt to redeploy resources is likely to encounter resistance however justified the decision in managerial or professional terms. Birmingham Social Services Department discovered this to their cost when they attempted to close Quinton Hall, a large nineteenth-century workhouse utterly unsuitable for its use as a residential home for the elderly. A vigorous campaign was mounted by NUPE under the slogan 'Save Quinton Hall'. After industrial action, the departmental management was obliged to retreat from its original plans – although closure was eventually effected, the timescale of change was greatly extended.

Setting priorities

Confronted with standstill budgets, managers have two choices. They can either redeploy resources with the consequent problems (if that involves closures) which Birmingham experienced in acute form, or they can ration services. The DHSS circular on rate fund expenditure issued in December 1974 identified priorities for social services as:

'(a) children at risk of ill-treatment.

(b) the very elderly or severely handicapped living alone – especially those recently discharged from hospital, recently bereaved or in inadequate housing.

(c) the mentally handicapped or mentally ill in urgent need of residential or day care, or domiciliary support, to prevent deterioration in their condition or to relieve intolerable strain on their families.

(d) vulnerable individuals, or families with vulnerable members, who are at imminent risk of breakdown under severe stress imposed on them by handicap, illness, homelessness or poverty.'

It was commented at the time that any self-respecting social worker could include virtually every client in these categories. Yet in subsequent years the guidance given by central government has become less and less specific, as under the banner of localized decision-making governments have abandoned any attempt at identifying where cuts should be made.

In 1976 the DHSS published a major planning statement, *Priorities for Health and Personal Social Services* (DHSS 1976), which identified priority groups with target growth rates for individual services. Changed economic conditions led to a further retreat from the form of indicative planning.

The most recent expression of the government's thinking is contained in *Care in Action*, a DHSS publication which is neither a consultative document nor a formal statement of priorities and bears the subtitle 'A handbook of policies and priorities for the Health and Personal Social Services in England' (DHSS 1981a). This continues the policy of identifying priority groups – the elderly, the mentally ill, the mentally handicapped, and the physically and sensorily handicapped – and priority services – those related to the care of children at risk and to the care and treatment of young offenders – which effectively cover the entire clientele of social services departments. It does not undertake the invidious task of identifying which sector of spending should be cut in order to develop services to these groups.

In this vacuum, a number of local authorities have attempted to define more precise criteria but significantly they have avoided the selection of specific client groups. The emphasis of such schemes has usually been either the element of risk in the situation or the statutory nature of the social work responsibilities. For example the priority scheme adopted by Bradford in 1975 placed as top priority those situations in which people are in actual physical or moral danger, and in a second category all the other statutory responsibilities of social services. Such schemes were of little help to fieldworkers confronted by a demanding client whose needs could not be met. What they did, however, was provide committee backing for the non-provision of services to certain groups of clients.

The British Association of Social Workers initially set itself squarely against any delineation of priorities. An emergency resolution at its 1974 Annual General Meeting rejected any 'concept of cuts in expenditure on one deprived group at the expense of another deprived group,' and urged the government to look to fields other than social services – education, health, and housing – for their major economies. The association's thinking had moved on by 1976 when it produced a detailed paper on priorities (Bamford 1976). While stressing that any attempt at definition and ranking inevitably led to invidious distinctions, the policy statement accepted that the gravity of the need presented by the client should be the major factor in weighing whether or not to intervene. An individual assessment on the basis of need was regarded as more equitable than rigid adherence to defined categories. And it was on that basis that area teams have worked to refine their own priority systems. The result of some of those efforts will be further considered in Chapter 3.

Child care tragedies

Coping with cuts, determining priorities, and dealing with conflict placed demands on management in social services, and called into question the quality of some managers. Yet more dramatic in their public impact were the seemingly endless series of child care tragedies and subsequent inquiries, and the initial round of cuts in public expenditure. Social workers trained in the last five years are all too aware of the reality of public scrutiny in the event of any injury to children for whom they have a responsibility. Yet when the inquiry into the life and death of Maria Colwell took place in 1973, it was a brutal shock to the social work system. Formerly, social workers and probation officers had laboured away, sometimes dismissed as impotent do-gooders but never subject to sustained doubts about their competence or their value to society. The public hearings of the Inquiry into Maria Colwell's supervision displayed the full extent of society's ambivalence about the powers held by social workers. The unfortunate social worker in the case was treated by the public as if she herself had struck the blows which killed Maria. The report (Colwell Report 1974) documented a sorry story of miscommunication, missed warning signals, and plain muddle, but it was the report's perception of managerial responsibility that is particularly noteworthy.

The report said explicitly that it would be impossible, and unfair, to lay the blame for the inadequacies in the care and supervision of Maria on any individual or group of individuals. Many of the mistakes were the result of, or contributed to, by inefficient systems operating in several different fields – training, administration, planning, liaison, and supervision. On five specific issues, the Social Services Department was held to be blameworthy. Denis Allen, the widely respected Director of East Sussex, made it clear to the inquiry that he accepted full responsibility for the actions of the social workers involved. Yet the report, the media coverage and the public reaction exposed the limitations to this notion of directorial responsibility. The individual social worker was clearly the person identified as bearing primary responsibility for the decisions and actions taken in relation to Maria. It is that sense of personal exposure – a sense vividly conveyed in the use in Stevenson's minority report of the phrase 'There, but for the grace of God, go I' – which has produced some hostile attitudes to management from staff who feel themselves unsupported in the front line (Colwell Report 1974: 8).

While Mr Allen had placed himself four-square with his staff, some of the Directors, later to endure the stress of a thorough-going investigation, were less ready to place themselves in the line of fire. And as the reports accumulated, the fire concentrated upon social workers and their first-line managers. 'More support and supervision by a senior social worker was necessary,' said the Review Body to enquire into the case of Stephen Meurs (Meurs Report 1975: 19); 'we would urge senior staff who carry responsibility for standards of professional practice constantly to remind social workers and others of the importance which should be attached to recording and to give practical help and supervision to secure an improvement in standards,' said the Darryn Clarke report (Clarke Report 1979: 58); 'the responsibility for carrying individual cases is so heavy that supervision needs to be built into the system,' said the Stephen Menheniott report (Menheniott Report 1978: 29).

The most explicit statement of the responsibilities of first-line managers is to be found in the Report of the Committee of Inquiry into the death of John Auckland. This stated:

'we consider that if a social services department is notified of a family where a child may be at risk the matter should not be considered initially at a level below that of a senior social worker who is a team leader. At regular intervals the case file of a family where the child may be at risk should be read by a senior worker who should then discuss the case with the social worker responsible and initial the file. Once there is cause for anxiety a social worker should immediately inform a senior social worker and no decision about care proceedings should be taken below a senior social worker level or even perhaps area officer level. The decision to close a file or render it inactive should not be taken by anyone below the level of senior social worker and the decisions and the reasons for it should be recorded on the file.'   (Auckland Report 1975: 88–90)

This extract is a good illustration of the emphasis on procedures that was the bureaucratic response to widespread public concern about child abuse. The creation of Area Review Committees and the development of registers meant that each local authority was obliged to review its procedures, and to lay down clear guidelines for practitioners. This had the effect of affording a secure framework for social workers carrying the onerous responsibility of supervising child abuse cases. Yet the insecurity of relatively inexperienced first-line and middle managers meant that the framework was not used as the means to develop good professional practice including responsible and planned risk-taking. Instead the desire for self-protection, always strong in bureaucracies like local authorities, came to the fore with great emphasis placed on compliance with procedures. This is not to argue that procedures are unnecessary or ineffective, but procedural safeguards protect only the agency. It is effective practice which can safeguard children and families, and at times the balance has tilted too far towards controls and procedural checks.

Effectiveness

One priority which did attract management attention was the need to demonstrate the effectiveness of social work intervention. When social work time was a secure resource, the pressure was on management to deploy that resource where it would do most good either by improving the client's emotional, physical, or social situation or, more prosaically but equally helpfully, by arresting further deterioration. The shared belief was that social work was an effective means of bringing about changes, but that belief was questioned in the latter half of the 1970s by increasingly strident critics of the pretensions of social work.

Halmos's famous work, *The Faith of the Counsellors* (Halmos 1965), described the emergence of the shared value systems of the counsel-ling professions as, in part, a result of the slump in the credibility of political solutions. Yet counselling in the form of social work practice remained essentially an act of faith in the absence of any empirical evidence of its efficacy in achieving desired results. To practitioners – to believers – it was a self-evident proposition that lower caseloads, affording more time for the healing qualities of personal relationships to be deployed, would lead to better outcomes. Unhappily the research evidence to support this proposition has been scanty, and the cries that 'The emperor has no clothes' have become more insistent.

The review of studies of social work effectiveness undertaken by Fischer (1976) suggested that not only was social work ineffective, but in several studies clients receiving services from professional social workers were shown to deteriorate. The major British study, IMPACT, provided devastating evidence that reducing the case-loads of probation officers had no significant impact on the outcomes of clients on a number of indicators (Folkard 1975 and 1976). The IMPACT study was significant because, unlike other UK studies, it could not easily be explained away as using the wrong measures, for the research study carried out over a number of years, supported and advised by probation staff and evaluating on several criteria, was as methodologically sound as any research study can be. Yet although the evidence of IMPACT was devastating, the effect on the probation service has belied the acronym of the project. It is true that there is greater scepticism abroad about the value of case-work undiluted by intervention in the social environment of the client, but the fundamental *modus operandi* of the majority of probation officers has altered little. It remains firmly based on a one-to-one contact.

The IMPACT study has had even less effect in other branches of social work. Sheldon has written critically of the unrivalled ability of social workers to disregard research:

> 'These findings are either not "believed" or they are seen as the products of a process which has little direct relevance to the practice situation. The chosen indicators of such critical studies never seem the "right" or "fair" ones in retrospect. Rumours circulate about alleged inadequacies in methodology, but perhaps the real fault in this kind of research is that the findings are distantly generated and often follow from research designs which the prac-titioners have had to "squeeze" themselves into rather than the reverse accommodation.'   (Sheldon 1978)

Yet even when the IMPACT study was closely aligned with prac-titioners from its inception, its findings have failed to affect practice.

But academic critics from within the profession writing in social work's own journals were a very different proposition to the criticism from outside the profession, which was making itself heard in the late 1970s. The succession of child care tragedies had created a climate of unease about the pretensions of social work, the chill economic climate meant that previously sacrosanct areas of public spending came under scrutiny, and the rightward shift of the political spectrum meant that social work, identified with radical views on the political process, came under attack. Patrick Jenkin, the incoming Secretary of State for Social Services, jibed that social workers were in danger of being mistaken for the Socialist Workers Party. And in the persons of Brewer and Lait, social work encountered the sternest challenge to its credibility.

Brewer and Lait are prolific writers. The *Daily Telegraph*, *Daily Mail*, and *The Spectator* were the chosen venues for their attacks on social work, expressing sentiments which evoked a warm editorial response. Their polemics were eventually drawn together in a book provocatively entitled *Can Social Work Survive?* (Brewer and Lait 1980). The essence of the argument deployed by Brewer and Lait is that social work has no coherent knowledge base, that it is ineffective in practice and that its training is unrealistic. As a consequence social services departments (they argue) are in disarray due to their over-ambitious and loosely formulated aims. It is a powerful polemic expressed with characteristic hyperbole.

The solutions proferred by Brewer and Lait are notably flimsy. They appear to envisage the relegation of social work to a paramedical activity, but clearly under medical control, without at any time addressing themselves to the problems which this would create. In truth, the book is not intended as an academic treatise. It has been ruthlessly dissected in reviews by Fischer (1981) and Sheldon (1982), two of the social work writers for whom they have a kind word. Its importance is as a populist statement of the mounting disquiet about social work.

This gloomy picture of the post-Seebohm decade may be thought to have little direct relevance to the task of social work management. Yet for those whose experience spans the decade, the bleak context here described is at the very heart of the management task. For social work has undergone a dramatic mood swing from the halcyon days when all things seemed possible, when resources were available in plenty and problems seemed soluble, to the present stage when management effort is devoted to protecting existing services from further cuts, and ensuring that the low morale of staff is not reflected in their work.

The skills which they require to operate in this changing environment are the subject of the chapters which follow. They include skill in communication, talent in deploying resources and supporting staff, clarity of thought and readiness to take responsibility for decisions. But managers need to be sensitive to the wider context within which they operate, for even if they wish to they cannot insulate themselves from the impact of social change.

3

Accountability and workload management

Much nonsense is talked and written about accountability in social work. The term is used synonomously with responsibility and prefaced by words like personal or professional – adjectives which do not necessarily lend the clarity that might be wished. Chapter 1 touched upon the importance of these concepts for managers, and discussed some of the difficulties which changes in the political and social environment have created in relation to the application of these ideas. It is important therefore to define the terms and the most helpful analysis is to be found in the Second Report of the Joint Steering Group on Accreditation in Social work (BASW 1980b).

The report identifies five different but related forms of accountability.

First, *personal accountability*: this is an important but often overlooked aspect. Essentially it is summed up in the phrase 'to thine own self be true'. It recognizes that each individual has his own set of values and beliefs against which he will measure his actions.

Second, *accountability to employer*: employees are accountable to their employer for the performance of their work in accordance with the policies and procedures laid down by the employer. Nevertheless in undertaking their work, staff are expected to apply the knowledge and skill which they have acquired through training and experience. In social work, as in other areas where professional skills are involved, the employee is expected to exercise discretion. It is in the exercise of that discretion that the employee brings to bear his knowledge and skill. Accountability to employers does not give employing agencies total freedom to determine their policies and procedures. In some instances the profession will appropriately seek to influence the policies within employing agencies.

Third, *professional accountability*: members of a profession experience the unity and sense of allegiance to shared value systems that come from a common knowledge base. As a consequence, they have a responsibility to see that their knowledge and skills are properly utilized. Some professions – law and medicine – are so regulated that the profession itself takes disciplinary action against those who fall short of expected standards. BASW has a Disciplinary Board, but rarely uses it. The proposal for a General Social Work Council with responsibility for accreditation would greatly strengthen this aspect of accountability.

Fourth, *accountability to other agencies for whom work is done*: the patterns of accountability vary significantly in different social work settings. Hospital-based social workers are accountable to the Social Services Committee for social work support to the National Health Service, not to the hospital in which they work. In contrast, probation officers have a dual accountability to their agency setting but also to the courts and prison department settings in which they work. The distinction appears to rest on the policy pursued by the employing agency, which defines the nature of accountability.

Fifth, *public accountability*: while in one sense public accountability is inherent in the nature of employment in local and central government, employees on occasion have a more direct experience. Public attitudes and press campaigns do establish limits on social workers' behaviour. Although misreported, the furore in Birmingham over the alleged placement of a child with a convicted prostitute is an illustration of how these limits are set.

Excluded from the forms of accountability listed in the report of the Joint Steering Group, and only partially subsumed within them, is *accountability to the client*. BASW's report, *Clients Are Fellow Citizens* (BASW 1980a), has focused professional attention directly on the issue of the rights of clients. While the accountability to clients is not direct in public social welfare agencies (in the sense that a client cannot discharge one worker and opt for another), there is increasing emphasis on the rights of clients to have a second opinion to challenge the discretionary powers of agencies, and to share more fully in decision-making. This new approach of openness, in many instances sharing with the client the contents of case files, does add a new dimension to traditional views of accountability.

Accountability can be defined as the determination of responsibility in accord with formal structures. But this narrow definition of accountability from line management relationships is not wholly adequate in terms of an analysis of social work, because of the intrusion of personal, professional, and public considerations. The complex structure of most large social work agencies does not lend itself to clear-cut statements of accountability. As a consequence it is not surprising to find considerable confusion. In their study of practitioners in area teams, Parsloe and Stevenson provide several such examples. 'I'm not quite sure how accountability works. In theory, since it's a hierarchical structure accountability should go right to the top, but in practice I don't think it really does'; and 'The ultimate responsibility I think is to the department, but . . . if you asked me to which particular person, I don't know'; and again 'Well, it's like saying "who are your employers?" I mean, where does it stop? I suppose with the general public who pay my salary through the rates. I think it goes all the way up – me, then [my head of department] and up through the hierarchy. But the buck would come here, oh yes, it would' (Parsloe and Stevenson 1978: p. 218). This acute contrast between clarity about personal responsibility and confusion about formal accountability suggests that agencies (to use Parsloe's words) have failed effectively 'to develop structures and managerial techniques which offered, in the words of one social worker, "protection with autonomy"' (Parsloe and Stevenson 1978: 224).

The relationship between professional practice and organizational structures has been helpfully clarified by work undertaken at Brunel University. Rowbottom and his colleagues (BIOSS 1974) distinguish between 'delegated discretion' and 'professional autonomy', arguing that social workers in fact exercise the former. Where powers are vested by statute either in the committee or the Chief Officer, the individual worker is indeed exercising delegated discretion in his practice, but it may feel like autonomy especially if he suspects that management will disown his judgements if they subsequently prove erroneous. Where, by statute, the powers rest directly with the individual, as in probation supervision, then the professional autonomy is complete although the probation officer is still accountable both to the courts and to his managers for his actions.

If, as Parsloe judges, the task of offering protection with autonomy has yet 'to be achieved', are there any guidelines for managers to follow in their quest for this elusive balance? It is important first to look at the differing ways in which area officers and team leaders can offer protection, and to examine how the commitment to 'democracy' and participative management can best be reconciled with the managerial responsibility to control the pattern and quality of service to the community. The studies undertaken as part of the DHSS research project (Parsloe and Stevenson 1978) found little evidence of any systematic planning by supervisors to acquaint themselves with information about all the cases being supervised by individual social workers. Many workers received no formal supervision. Little attention was given to formal delineation of priorities at team level. Overall, there was very little control exercised over social workers' practice, in striking contrast to the tight control over all other resources.

The starting point for any managerial control has to be knowledge of the size of the workload. In pre-Seebohm days, many social workers carried huge caseloads (up to 200) but knew well that volume itself was a poor indicator of workload. The demands which cases make on the worker's time and skills vary greatly. An apparently straight-forward referral of an old person needing a bath aid may involve the worker in liaison with a network of services – both health and personal social services – may necessitate the creation of a supporting group of helpers and volunteers, may require skilled social work in helping the elderly client to accept the fact of his increasing infirmity and dependence, and may eventually lead the worker to become involved in assessing suitability for admission to residential care, *or* it may lead to only a single contact and supply of the aid sought. On a caseload count, both cases weigh equally. The obvious shortcomings of this approach have caused its abandonment. The irony is that recognition of the problems seems to have led many managers to give up the effort of getting to know the size and nature of their social workers' caseloads. That is an abdication of responsibility, for without that knowledge, managers can offer no help to their staff in regulating the flow of work appropriately.

There are a number of ways in which managers can become more directly engaged in controlling the workload for their team. Four differing approaches are considered below. Caseload management

systems, the case review system developed by Goldberg and colleagues (Goldberg and Warburton 1979), operational and other
priority systems, and management by objectives.

Caseload management

The study carried out by the research team headed by Parsloe and
Stevenson (1978) found only a very patchy awareness of systems of
regulating caseloads to make allowance for differential complexity.
Much appeared to depend on whether a member of staff had attended
a course at the National Institute for Social Work. The work developed by Vickery (1977) at NISW has had substantial influence on
practice. It deals only with caseloads, not with total workload. It has
nevertheless considerable value to managers.

The initial phase advocated is a total review of the entire caseload,
determining which cases should be closed, which should be handled
differently, and which should be continued in the same way. Vickery
suggests that a concomitant of this review should be an explicit
statement of why a case should remain open. The criteria that she
proposes reflect the influence of those who argue that the efficacy of
intervention should be a major determinant. They are:

(a) Where the client has a problem which can be solved or ameli-
     orated in a reasonable period of time.
(b) Where the client's problem is insoluble, but it is causing distress
     to others who can benefit from support, or where further de-
     terioration will occur without support.
(c) Where clients are vulnerable and lack close connections with
     family, friends or other supportive networks.
(d) Where clients need adequate preparation for dealing with a
     problem likely to arise.
(e) Where clients have apparently intractable problems, but provide
     an opportunity for social workers to try new methods.

That review takes time. When an agency is under pressure, time is a
scarce commodity. But without a thorough review, it is not possible
for both supervisor and social worker to be satisfied that all the cases
carried are on the caseload for a realistic purpose. Vickery argues that
regardless of the client's willingness to enter into a 'contract' with the
social worker, it is essential for the worker to state clearly on the

record what is to be achieved. She identifies eight components to recording. These are:

(1) *Problem definition:* this should include the social worker's definition, but also perceptions of the problem by the client, his family, or the referring agency where these differ.

(2) *Goals:* these should be the outcomes sought as a result of social work intervention, and should be stated in behavioural terms. Thus clearing of debts, finding a job, or attending school regularly are acceptable formulations, but 'an improved level of social functioning' would not be.

(3) *People to be influenced:* here the influence of the unitary approach becomes evident. In addition to the client, there are other significant figures in the environment who may need to be influenced – target systems in the jargon of the unitary method.

(4) *People to be involved in exerting influence:* while in some instances only the social worker is involved, the more frequent pattern is that other workers also exercise influence on the client, e.g. teachers, volunteers, residential workers – action systems.

(5) *Methods of exerting influence, and roles and activities of the worker:* again Vickery argues a specific statement of activities rather than a global formulation. If the methods and activities are specific, it should be possible to predict the amount of time which the case is likely to absorb.

(6) *Frequency of contact needed with client and/or others in relation to the goals to be achieved:* this is the most difficult area for those using this approach. Workers are required to classify each case according to the goal currently requiring the highest frequency of contact. The classification here is not of the client, but of the case goal, and is thus subject to change.
  The classification utilized is:

  (a) Behavioural change. Contact: weekly or more.
  (b) Support or maintenance of a social situation. Contact: 2–4 weeks.
  (c) Personal maturation. Contact: several times weekly.
  (d) Responding to a crisis. Contact: substantial over a short period.
  (e) Environmental change and provision of practical/material help. Contact: estimate must be calculated on the basis of

local knowledge.
(f) Reassessing client situations. Contact: as required.
(g) Assessment. Contact: as much as may be required to formu-
     late goals and plans for intervention.

(7) *Resources of time needed for work that is not direct contact with client or
    others:* this covers the elements of work on behalf of the client
    which do not involve direct contact. It thus includes time spent on
    travelling, recording, report-writing, telephone calls, etc. Work-
    ers are required to estimate the amount of time involved on the
    basis of their knowledge of the client and the environment.
(8) *Likely length of the case:* in some instances, for example hospital
    social work or a supervision order, there may be a time limit to
    contact imposed by the context. Vickery advocates for purposes
    of caseload management that 'it is better to work intensively for a
    short time, review progress, and, if possible, close the case rather
    than to drag on with an ever-increasing load of clients for whom
    very little is achieved.'

These items 1–8 should then be recorded on a form, which provides
the basis for estimating the time involved in meeting the needs of the
client. The worker then aggregates the time needed to meet the needs
of the total caseload, and plots this over a four-week period. Vickery
suggests a form which lists clients, goals, contact planned, time
needed for other work, and also leaves space for new clients or new
goals emerging in relation to existing clients.

The supervisor is thus able to see how the worker's commitments
match with time available. By monitoring how actual contact over a
four-week period accords with plans, difficulties experienced by the
worker in managing time can be seen virtually at a glance. A clear
picture is available of the workload demands presented by different
clients. The allocation of cases can be decided on the basis of accurate
information both about the size and nature of the worker's caseload.

The advantages to the supervisor of this method are considerable,
but its implementation presents difficulties. It requires time, and the
ready support of the staff involved. The argument that social workers
are too busy to spend their time filling forms strikes at the jugular of
the manager, already ambivalent about being enmeshed in bureaucratic processes. And the power of the argument is reinforced by the

explicit appeal to guilt, 'I need to spend my time with my clients.' The introduction of such a scheme will therefore require careful nego-tiation, a proposition which applies with equal force to the other methods considered below of giving a greater sense of direction and purpose to the supervisory process.

The model is limited in its potential application. It is designed in such a way as to meet the needs of long-term work, and needs major modification if it is to be used for all referrals. Many such referrals involve only short-term work. Goldberg and Warburton (1979) found 47 per cent of referrals were closed within one week.

Like all categorization systems, the dividing line between categor-ies is not always clear. The frequency of contact envisaged within the classification system too is open to question. Thus the required contact of several times weekly for clients whose need is categorized as personal maturation may be valid for inadequate parents, the par-ticular example cited, but excessive for a troubled adolescent. Inevi-tably too the proposed frequency of contact reflects a view of existing norms in agencies. Yet these norms reflect existing levels of staffing and are subject to change. For example, an agency required to cut staff may reduce the frequency of visiting of some client categories. That policy will however be based on categories, whether of client or problem, which are unrelated to Vickery's classification.

Inevitably there will be different perceptions about the value of the method. Used consistently by a team committed to the model, it should have a considerable impact on practice by securing a higher level of clarity about the objectives being sought and the time involvement required to achieve them.

Case review system

This was developed by staff at the National Institute for Social Work as a means of establishing systematic record and review systems which would enable social workers to establish the problems they were trying to tackle, the means employed, and the objectives of inter-vention. The genesis of the scheme arose from the widespread recog-nition that social workers experienced acute difficulties in formulating plans, and tended to hold on to cases even when no specific objective was being furthered by continued contact with the clients.

The form developed through the research is fully described

(Goldberg and Warburton 1979) in a detailed account of the case review system and the findings of the workload analysis arising from the use of the review form. It is important here to note that following the experiment in Southampton, the DHSS funded an extended research project on the use of the form in Cambridgeshire. There have been some modifications to the original form as a result of the longer experience, but the basic structure remains intact with categorization of practical services, outstanding client problems, social worker activities, and explicit goals. It will at once be clear that the thinking underlying the system is closely akin to the caseload management model developed by Vickery.

The form requires social workers to tick the appropriate boxes, indicating changes since the last review and services or activities planned before the next review. In sequence, therefore, the review forms relating to any client provide a record of how faithfully activities followed the plan, of their impact, and of future plans. The activities section of the form details all the practical services or tangible changes in the situation which have occurred since the last review or are planned for the near future. These range from domiciliary services like home help and meals on wheels, to changes in circumstances like discharge from care or a change of legal status. In addition, the type of worker dealing with the case is listed as are those outside agencies in contact with the client.

The categorization of social worker activities is rather different from that used in the Vickery model. The categories used describe the nature of social work activities rather than the case goal. They include assessment activity, information/advice, mobilizing resources, advocacy, education in social skills, check-up/review visiting, facilitating problem-solving/decision-making, sustaining/nurturing, and group activities. The social work activities planned should relate to a section of the case review form headed 'future'. In this section, workers are asked to specify in narrative form those changes which they are seeking, and to identify the major change area sought. These are categorized as no change, major environmental, social/personal environment, social role, and behaviour/attitude/relationships.

Before proceeding to the 'future', workers have to categorize the present problems of the client. These range from those associated with client group membership – elderly, mental illness, mental handicap – to specific problem areas – employment, transport, and housing.

Again the worker has to indicate problems tackled since the last review and those present at this review.

The claims advanced for the case review system are fivefold. First, it can help social workers to evaluate and plan their work. Second, it can be used as an educational tool to assist the supervision process. Third, it helps management better to plan fieldwork services by indicating the balance of problems from different client groups, the time investment required to meet them adequately, and the most effective deployment of staff. Fourth, it provides a continuing source of information about social work activities for use both with individual workers and by the general public. Fifth, it facilitates further research into the efficacy of social work intervention.

These advantages are dependent on the commitment of social workers and their supervisors to comprehensive and conscientious completion of the review form. Even in Cambridgeshire with the 'halo' effect of involvement in a research project, opinions about the utility of the system are divided. The basic objection to the time involved is similar to that used against the Vickery caseload management model. Nevertheless 60 per cent of social workers felt that the system was worth the effort involved. Disappointingly the use of the case review system outside the areas participating in the research project has been very limited. If it is to be more widely adopted – whether in tandem with the Vickery model or independently – a more analytical approach to problems will have to be built into social work training so that newly appointed social workers have some familiarity with the techniques required.

Operational priority system

This approach (OPS) was developed by Hall (1975). It provides a forum in which policy decisions are made explicit at a local level and which recognizes the crucial role of the fieldworker in implementation of policies within the broad parameters laid down by the department. The system involves the construction of a chart consisting of five columns headed, respectively: problem; minimum adequate response; maximum feasible response; maximum desirable response; incidence. By minimum adequate response is understood the response that would be given if the case were seen as low priority, while maximum feasible response represents the response if the case were accorded high priority. Unlike the other systems described above, this system also provides for specification of the appropriate response if there were no resource constraints either of staffing or money. It thus facilitates the identification of any shortfall as well as constituting a statement of long-term objectives.

In an account of the application of OPS in an area team, Whitmore and Fuller (1980) list ten problem categories which together made up over 90 per cent of referrals. They were:

(1) Families where children are at risk:
    (a) suffering or in danger of non-accidental injury;
    (b) suffering emotional abuse/neglect;
    (c) suffering or in danger of physical neglect.
(2) Families with environmental problems:
    (a) financial – (i)   fuel bills,
                   (ii)   rent/mortgage arrears,
                   (iii) clothing/household equipment,
                   (iv) not enough money;
    (b) housing – (i)   homelessness,
                  (ii)   poor conditions.
(3) Children in trouble:
    (a) anti-social behaviour involving –
                (i)   disruptive behaviour in school, home and/or community,
                (ii)   delinquency;
    (b) unhappy child.
(4) Living alone (elderly and/or physically handicapped):
    (a) physical difficulties in carrying out household task, shopping, etc.;
    (b) budgeting/financial difficulties;
    (c) social isolation.
(5) Resource finding:
    (a) recruitment of foster parents;
    (b) recruitment of playgroup supervisors/child minders;
    (c) stimulating good neighbour schemes;
    (d) recruitment of specialist volunteers for families;
    (e) improving voluntary transport provision;
    (f) group-work with adolescents (informal);
    (g) groups for mothers and pre-school children;

    (h) groups for primary school age children after school;
    (i)   recruitment of home helps;
    (j)   obtaining day care.

(6) Families where there is an elderly relative:
    (a) elderly person has difficulty in carrying out household tasks/shopping;
    (b) relationship problem between elderly person and other family members.

(7) Problems associated with mental handicap:
    (a) families with mentally handicapped child under five;
    (b) families with mentally handicapped child of school age;
    (c) mentally handicapped school leavers;
    (d) mentally handicapped adults.

(8) Families with physically handicapped member:
    (a) physically handicapped child;
    (b) adult with sudden onset of handicap;
    (c) adult with long-term progressive handicap.

(9) Blind and partially sighted:
    (a) blind children;
    (b) adult/elderly blind;
    (c) adult/elderly partially sighed.

(10) Adoption:
    (a) adoption agency work – (i)   work with natural parents,
                             (ii) placement duties,
                             (iii) approval of prospective adopters;
    (b)   (i)   adoption welfare supervision,
                             (ii) guardian *ad litem* duties.

(It is a sad reflection of the relative neglect of the mentally ill by social services departments that there is no category covering the mentally disordered.)

Each sub-category has the three levels of response referred to above. As an illustration, the levels of response for the problem category 'living alone (elderly and/or physically handicapped)' are reproduced in *Table (3)1*.

A crucial feature in the system is measurement of the incidence of the problem. This enables managers to identify pressure points where

Table 3(1) *Extract from operational priority chart*

Problem	Minimum adequate response	Maximum feasible response	Maximum desirable response	Incidence (six month period)
(4) Living alone (physically handicapped and elderly)				
(a) Physical difficulties in carrying out household chores, shopping etc.	(a) Visit by OT and/or HHO – plus follow-up liaison with GP	(a) Assessment visit by HHO/OT/SW includes decision whether other worker involvement is necessary. Monitored contact to day care (E + PH/E). Liaison with good neighbour scheme in certain parts of the area. Liaison with housing if necessary. Provision of aids to living, home help. Liaison with GP/HV district nurse. Provision of Part III when necessary. Short stay Part III. CSDP registration. Meals on wheels if necessary.	(a) Assessment visit by HHO/OT includes decision whether SW involvement is necessary. Provision of aids to living, home help. Monitored contact to day care (E + PH). Monitored contact with good neighbour scheme. Provision of sheltered workshop (PH). Provision of adequate transport. Facilities to make above possible. Liaison with housing if necessary. Liaison with GP/HV district nurse. Provision of Part III when necessary.	224

(b) Budgeting/financial difficulties.	(b) Liaison with DHSS/Inland Revenue/WWDC (Rates). Supportive letter to local charity.	(b) Advocacy. Financial advice by SW/HH etc. Supportive letter to local charities.	(b) Advocacy. Financial advice by SW/HH etc. Supportive letter to local charities.	18
(c) Social isolation (geographical and/or feeling isolated)	(c) Assessment visit by social worker plus contact of relatives, if any. Visit if necessary by handicraft instructress.	(c) Assessment visit by social worker plus contact of relatives if any. Monitored contact to day care (E + PH/E). Monitored contact with PHAB Club (PH). Introduction to social clubs (E). Liaison with housing if necessary. Liaison with good neighbour scheme in certain parts of the area. Visit by handicraft instructress if necessary.	(c) Assessment visit by social worker plus contact of relatives if any. Monitored contact to day care (E + PH). Monitored contact with PHAB Club (PH). Monitored contact with good neighbour scheme. Introduction to social clubs. Liaison with housing if necessary. Provision of Tel/TV under CSD Act 1970. Provision of sheltered workshop. Provision of adequate transport to make above possible. Visit by handicraft instructress if necessary.	14

additional resources may be needed as well as those areas where skills are being under-utilized. Thus – like the other two systems discussed – OPS gives managers additional means of controlling the flow of work, and the essential information required to plan services effectively. In their discussion of the application of the system, Whitmore and Fuller (1980) identify the difficulty of securing consistency of response as a major problem faced by the team. A substantial input of time in preliminary discussion and checking of responses is necessary. The very act of making explicit choices and explaining them was found to be helpful by opening up for team discussion the underlying values and concepts of the individual workers. Although the concept of time is not built in to this approach, Whitmore and Fuller argue that by examining retrospectively a number of pieces of work at one level it should be possible to quantify the approximate time needed to complete a task.

The weakness of the OPS approach is that while it is geared to the needs of the client it views available responses entirely from the perspective of the agency and its workers. The consumer perspective of the maximum feasible response is lacking, although in theory it should be possible to carry out a study of consumer opinion and test the findings against the workers' perceptions.

Priority systems

Reference was made in Chapter 2 to the formal adoption of priority systems by some local authorities. In 1976, BASW reviewed and commented upon the early attempts to establish priorities between referrals, and detailed work has subsequently been undertaken by Algie and others (Algie 1975; Algie and Miller 1976; Bamford 1976; Algie, Hey, and Mallen 1981).

The initial efforts to set priorities were somewhat crude. They emphasized first the legal basis of intervention and as subsidiary factors the element of risk involved, risk of physical or moral danger, or risk of damage to others, but frequently included as a secondary priority those cases where social work intervention was likely to prove effective. Northamptonshire's scheme at the time, for example, expressly wrote into one priority category:

'and it is predictable that the action which the department is able to take will change the situation with one of the following results:

(i)   improvement will take place or
(ii)   deterioration will be avoided or
(iii) deterioration will be significantly slowed down.'

The overall impact of schemes was to give a high weighting to statutory work, which in effect meant child care work. It reinforced the tendency within agencies to emphasize child abuse cases and to make greater use of a legal framework when working with families at risk. Anomalously this could lead to an adolescent youth on a supervision order being given a higher priority than an elderly person finding increasing problems in coping with the everyday demands of life.

The influence of Algie and colleagues at the National Institute for Social Work on thinking about social services priorities has been substantial. They devised a framework for analysing and agreeing priorities using the concept of a client problem dictionary (Algie and Miller 1976). This is arranged in the form of a matrix with the horizontal axis dealing with client problems, and the vertical axis with the degree of severity of malfunctioning experienced by the client. This usually covers four levels of functioning: *vulnerable* where the client is potentially at risk but is able to cope unaided; *impaired* where the client's functioning is affected but where he is able to cope with assistance, although this need not come from a social services department; *deteriorated* where the level of functioning is worsening but can be ameliorated or stabilized with additional external assistance; and *collapsed* where full care, often necessitating residential admission, is required. Specific problem factors can be entered in the cells formed by the axes. An example in relation to physical handicap is shown in *Table 3(2)*.

Services available and problem severity can be matched in a similar matrix using the range of service options in the example of planning given by Whitmore and Fuller above. The existing level of service response to problems can then be assessed. But equipped with this detailed analysis, it remains necessary to balance the multiple elements and to determine the criteria to which most weight will be given. These include preventability, severity, resource availability, prevalence of needs, ease of administration, and a dozen others identified by Algie and Miller.

The conceptualization developed by Algie (1975) is sufficiently

Table 3(2) *Fieldwork priorities for handicapped clients*

Physical handicap	*Physical*	*Mental/emotional*	*Support systems*	*Occupation/finance/ housing*	*Social skills capability*
Vulner-able	Disability has altered role in work/family	Normal reactive depression/ anxiety/anger/ guilt	Willing but under constant pressure	Reduced capacity but working Housing just adequate	At times impaired by disability/immobility
Impeded	Partial dependency on others to cope with daily living Recurrent bouts of illness Condition slowly progressing	Depression/ hostility/fear impedes ability to adjust to limitations	Intermittently reliable Inappropriate at times	Housing exacerbates dependency Difficulties in finding employment Considerably reduced income	Requires some help to manage own affairs

Deterio-rated	Onset of acute or chronic illness increases dependency	Emotional break-down – talks of 'wishing to die'	Unreliable Uncaring Not physically or emotionally strong enough to cope	Too disabled to work in open employment Cannot be controlled in day centre Major debts Likelihood of homelessness/very unsuitable housing	Refusal to accept help to manage own affairs
Collapsed	Totally dependent terminally/acutely ill Grossly/multiply handicapped Bedridden	Suicidal Brain-damaged Paranoid	Total rejection of patient by family or vice versa	Unemployable Unoccupiable Homeless Immobile/housebound	Total breakdown in management of own affairs

broad to encompass both the operational priority and workload management systems considered earlier. They are however perhaps less daunting to practitioners than the complex web of matrices described by Algie. Nevertheless it is the language and concept of the client problem dictionary which underpins much discussion of field-work priorities in social services departments.

Management by objectives

This model, derived from management theory, offers a means of incorporating the use of contract theory and task-centred casework. The impact of *Brief and Extended Casework* (Reid and Shyne 1969) and *Task-Centred Casework* (Reid and Epstein 1972) on practice is reflected in this approach to managing the workload of a team or area. The key to management by objectives is clarity – clarity about the objectives required by the agency and about how performance in striving for those objectives will be measured.

Drucker, in the context of industrial management, wrote:

'each manager from the "big boss" down to the production fore-man needs clearly spelled out objectives. These objectives should lay out what performance the man's own managerial unit is supposed to produce. They should lay out what contribution he and his unit are expected to make to help other units obtain their objectives. Finally, they should spell out what contribution the manager can expect from other units towards the attainment of his own objectives. Right from the start, in other words, emphasis should be on team-work and team results.'

(Drucker 1955: 124)

Translated to a social work agency, this means that every manager from the director down to the individual social worker – who has the responsibility for managing time – must set objectives for himself, and set objectives where performance can be measured or observed. Social workers too often retreat into fine-sounding phrases about growth, understanding, and development which are not measurable. The task of formulating objectives in behavioural terms is difficult, but it is an integral element in this managerial approach.

The director of an agency might have a banner objective of improving social welfare services in the area. But defined behaviourally that objective might be measured by increased volume of service, by increased quality (although that presupposes MBO in force throughout the organization), or negatively by reduced volume of complaints. Other senior managers with a problem of under-utilized residential or day care resources might define their objectives in terms of increasing occupancy levels, or reducing the unit cost of provision. This exercise gives a precision to management, which helps both the manager and his staff. For the individual social worker this approach is expressed very much in terms of a contract between worker and client, which makes explicit the objectives of the relationship.

The DHSS study (Parsloe and Stevenson 1978) found this approach utilized in one team. For each client a 'contract form' was completed. This outlined the type of problem presented and the goals and method of intervention which formed the basis of a contract between worker and client. Each week 'planned' and 'achieved' aims were noted for each client. After three months each worker evaluated his cases by assessing aspects, e.g. the nature of the client's adjustment, on a five-point scale. The concept of contract is important in social work. It figures prominently in differing approaches to practice because it captures the consensual element which – except in probation and parole – has usually been regarded as the cornerstone of practice.

In their review of practitioners' comments about their work, Parsloe and Stevenson (1978) identify three broad categories used to describe the concept. First, some social workers regarded contract as synonomous with making explicit the goals of one's intervention. While clarity about goals is important, a true contract must also be openly shared with the client and modified by him. Curiously, some of those interviewed were reluctant to share their plans of intervention with clients while paying lip-service to the idea of contract. Second, as in the team considered above, there was a contractual basis to all work undertaken. The limitation on this was the difficulty experienced in getting clients' agreement to a course of action, especially when there was little motivation. Third, some workers utilized the theoretical concept by conducting open negotiations with clients about the purpose of intervention, time-scale involved, and the respective roles of worker and client. This latter group were often influenced by the task-centred formulation of Reid and Epstein (1972). The particular features of task-centred casework are the emphasis on planned, time-limited intervention, and on the client's part in accomplishing the task.

Workload management in the probation service

The rapid growth in the number of social enquiry reports undertaken by the probation service was the stimulus to re-examine how the flow of work could be controlled and managed. It was recognized that the pressure of meeting deadlines in order to satisfy the requirements of the courts meant that the practice of routine supervision, the everyday bread-and-butter activity which nevertheless constitutes the primary task of the service, was in danger of neglect. The National Association of Probation Officers undertook a study of workloads, drawing on American examples where a time value was given to each piece of work. The values given were based on judgement, rather than research. A trial of the system in twelve probation areas found an average working week of 44.6 hours in which officers were striving to complete an average of 51.4 units of work. The probation service has devoted considerable attention to workload measurement. There is a nationally agreed system in relation to monthly returns although it is perhaps significant that Home Office statistics still use a crude caseload count to record the level of activity. The National Activity Recording Study was intended to refine workload weightings. It has not done so for two reasons. First, any diary exercise can record only the worker's own perception of his activities, not always the most objective assessment. Second, the diversification taking place within the service into day centre activities, community liaison projects, and social skills training means that the former clusters of activities and weightings are no longer valid. Thus while the search for clarity of objectives remains valid, less attention is now being paid to the elusive search for workload measures.

Common features

Having considered a range of the methods used by team leaders in order to control the flow of work and to ensure the maintenance of standards, it is worth looking at the similar features of the various methods. The formalized priority categories based on client groups or client status have least in common with any of the other approaches. While providing fieldworkers with a managerially defined notion of priorities they do not help the daily flow of work unless management is willing to make explicit its inability to offer assistance. Except in emergencies, agencies are extremely reluctant to refuse any assistance – a tendency exacerbated in those authorities which regard the volume of referrals as an important indicator of demand. If for several years one has been seeking resources by pointing to the increasing number of referrals as evidence of need, a conscious policy of rejecting certain groups of referrals and thus over a period reducing the volume of demand invites politicians to draw certain conclusions.

The systems which look at clients individually, albeit grouping them into particular categories for conceptual purposes, seem more rewarding both to fieldworkers and to managers. The case review system, Vickery's caseload management model, the operational priority system, and management by objectives each require a full re-examination of every piece of work in progress. They each require the worker to be explicit about the goals of intervention and about the activities which he plans to undertake. In short, they require a discipline and a rigour which does not come naturally to most social workers. 'Social workers showed little interest or capacity to analyse their rationale for determining the frequency of contact nor whether it took place in the client's home or in the office. Social workers seemed to make such decisions without conscious thought.' This damning remark does not come from the Brewer and Lait (1980) study, but from Parsloe's discussion of the educational implications of the research study (Parsloe and Stevenson 1978: 339). The revolution in attitudes which the approaches discussed have to bring about is all too evident.

That revolution requires social work managers' active support. It is important to understand the reasons for resistance to a more disciplined approach. First, social workers are suspicious of managerial solutions. Some of the reasons for this were discussed in Chapter 1. They include the diminution of professional autonomy, the lack of support from management when an emergency occurs, the squeeze on resources, and the crisis of confidence within social work. Any attempt to secure greater knowledge of how social workers use their time may therefore well be seen as a bid to strengthen managerial control, and further to limit the independent decision-making of social workers.

Second, the systematic approach may be resisted because the very process of categorizing people, problems, and solutions is seen as a mechanistic process which ignores the need to individualize clients and their problems. This is an important argument advanced most persuasively by Wilkes (1981), who contends that as social workers and managers turn increasingly to purposive, task-centred, and goal-orientated methods in which effectiveness is a dominant criterion for intervention, there is a real danger that some groups will be neglected by social workers because their problems are less tractable and less well suited to speedy change. If support as a goal of intervention has been used too indiscriminately in the past, one must acknowledge that there is a group of clients for whom the availability of a non-judgemental worker can constitute the difference between survival and going under. The task of the manager is to differentiate between the great majority of clients, for whom a task-centred approach can provide an effective service, and those who need long-term support. In reality, however, there is little that is mechanistic about the various conceptual approaches which have been examined. Each contains the capacity for a flexible response to individual need.

Third, these systems are seen as a device to ration services. There is considerable truth in this. What they do, however, is to substitute a rational explicit process for an intuitive covert rationing process. As such they should be welcomed by radicals, for they are more open to challenge and change. The problem is that covert systems can be circumvented or ignored in certain situations, and that is more difficult when the rationing process is explicit.

Fourth, workload management systems are criticized for their failure fully to reflect the diversification of the social work role. While work with individual clients is important, the unitary approach stresses the importance of the worker's interaction with the social environment. Time spent in liaison with voluntary organizations or in mobilizing community networks may be more valuable than direct work, yet may be inadequately reflected in any weightings.

The approaches that have been considered relate to one aspect of the middle manager's task – getting to know the workload of the individual worker. The different approaches that can be deployed in the process of supervision itself are discussed in the following chapter.

Implications for accountability

Earlier the problems of affording 'protection with autonomy' were considered. The different approaches outlined above can now be tested against the sorry indictment of practice constituted by Parsloe's description of supervisory methods. The systematic examination of work required overcomes a major problem identified by Parsloe (Parsloe and Stevenson 1978), namely that many supervisors discussed only those cases which a worker elected to discuss. The emphasis on goals enables supervisors to assess the effectiveness of intervention from the client's perspective, but also the determination of the worker to pursue and carry through a particular approach. The overall picture of area needs available through the case review and operational priority systems helps the manager to formulate a policy to meet the total workload of the team. In particular, given the sensitivity of social workers to press and public criticism, a regular review enables managers to have early warning of situations which may cause subsequent problems and so require careful management. In such cases, a sharing of responsibility for difficult decisions can offer reassurance to inexperienced workers and – on occasion – to experienced workers also.

The examples used relate to social services departments and to their fieldwork services. It is in this context that the issues have been posed most acutely as a result of heightened public awareness of the responsibilities of social workers in a local authority setting. But it is not only the highly publicized child care cases which have raised issues of accountability. The bombardment of referrals – with an increase of up to 50 per cent between 1971 and 1975 according to Goldberg and Warburton's (1979) research, and with little slowing of that rate of increase in many urban areas in the latter half of the decade – created a state of confusion with which managers are still grappling. The managerial task in residential and day care work is somewhat different. While the problems posed are no less acute, they rarely constitute the lack of focus or clear objectives which these systems are designed to combat in fieldwork practice.

The different statutory basis from which probation officers operate has previously been considered. While personal responsibility is explicitly placed on the individual officer, and that is recognized by courts, offenders, and the probation service, in one sense the officer is even more constrained than his local authority counterpart. Unlike the broad range of responsibilities carried by social services departments, probation is – notwithstanding its continuing involvement in matrimonial jurisdiction – largely concerned with offenders. Unlike social services departments which have a confused albeit quite positive public image, the probation and after-care service is readily understood. It even provided source material for a popular ITV soap opera in the 1950s. The result is that the function of the agency itself constitutes a constraint. In the terms used in the discussion of accountability at the beginning of the chapter, probation officers have to exercise their skills with regard to their employing agency, and also the courts and prisons within which they work. While they may properly seek to reform these institutions, officers have to operate within the limits defined by agency function which require them to work in settings whose values may be alien to those of social work. This has limited the ability of probation officers to engage in preventive work without an individual focus, for instance with a delinquency-prone school. Some probation officers have initiated imaginative and innovative projects which go beyond the primary purpose of the agency, but have needed the backing of senior management to achieve this.

4

Supervision and staff development

In the previous chapter, the ways in which managers can regulate the flow of work and ensure that objectives are fulfilled were explored. While those techniques may constitute the machinery for effective management of staff, the practice of supervision is the means whereby this is achieved. Supervision has a slightly different meaning in the context of social work to that in everyday usage. While the dictionary defines supervision in terms of inspection and control, the exercise of authority over subordinates, social workers frequently refer to supervision in terms of a consultative process. In this process, the methods of work employed and the goals pursued by the worker may be discussed. The supervisor may try to influence the worker, but what is offered by the supervisor is advice and guidance rather than instruction. While perceptions are changing with a greater emphasis now being placed on managerial accountability, ten years ago the availability of good supervision was frequently used as a selling point by local authority advertisers seeking to recruit staff.

But describing supervision as an enabling process tends to mask the relationship between supervision and accountability. If discussion of methods and objectives takes place with a colleague of the same status, the activity is one of consultation. Supervision does imply a relationship of authority, although in social work the authority is tacit. One of the reasons for the development of this unusual approach to supervision is the importance of individual professional responsibility in social work. Hedged as it is by the qualifications discussed in

Chapter 3 the concept of individual responsibility continues to exercise a potent influence on the evolution of social work agencies. The process of supervision serves however to reinforce the worker's organizational accountability as well as to facilitate individual development. The supervisor, by assisting the individual worker, is also serving the needs of the agency by ensuring a higher level of performance.

The pattern of supervision discussed below is that widely used in fieldwork. Yet the principles and values discussed are equally applicable to residential settings. Where the work setting is the same as the client setting, as in residential work, there is a direct sharing of experiences between the residential worker and client, and also between the supervisor and the worker. It resembles 'live' supervision, where the supervisor both observes and participates in the interactions between worker and client.

Agency responsibilities

The attitude of the agency to supervision is critical. While the days have gone when the establishment of the conditions for good supervision was seen as a recruitment aid and a means of keeping staff, social work agencies do recognize the vital part which supervision can play in improving standards of practice. This recognition is important for without it supervision can easily be viewed as a self-indulgent leisurely re-examination of work already done when there are dozens of clients needing help. This attitude is sometimes displayed by those in managerial positions who are uncertain about their ability to cope with the anxieties of the worker, and by those workers unable to step back and critically examine their own practice. This latter group often prefer to immerse themselves in work. Files are piled high, diaries are constantly full, and yet real examination of the quality of the work being undertaken is lacking.

The agency meets its responsibility to facilitate supervision by the provision of physical space and by creating time for the supervisor to prepare, conduct, and reflect on supervision sessions. Space is often at a premium in crowded offices. Staffing growth over the last ten years means that once-adequate office accommodation is now cramped. Partly as a result of scarce financial resources, and partly as a result of worker preferences, many social workers work in an open-plan setting, with at least one team sharing a large room. The probation and after-care service, which traditionally has made much more use of office-based contact, retains individual offices as the norm, but in social services departments team leaders can frequently be found in the same room as the workers they supervise. Whatever the merits of open-plan design, it is inimical to social work supervision. This requires time for reflection and thought removed from the press of ringing phones, bustling colleagues, and the myriad distractions of a team room. Ideally the team leader should have a room of his own, but where physical constraints do not allow this, an interview room needs to be reserved for supervision use.

Time, like space, is at a premium in social work. The agency therefore has a responsibility to ensure that sufficient time is available for high-quality supervision. There are three aspects to the provision of time. First, and the most often overlooked, is adequate time for preparation. This means making time in a busy working week to read the case material to be discussed in the supervision session. Second, the setting aside on a regular basis time for uninterrupted supervision sessions. Third, allowing the supervisor time to make notes on the supervision session and time to think about its implications. The importance of thinking time both before and after supervision can hardly be overstated yet this is the aspect of supervision which frequently goes by default under work pressures.

While these three aspects of agency responsibility may seem obvious to some, it is striking how often they are ignored. The practice of supervision 'on demand' has replaced the regular supervision session as the norm in many social work teams. With open-plan offices and all referrals passing through the team leader, it is argued that the most effective supervision is the immediate discussion of problems presented in work with clients. This 'demand feeding' has three detrimental results. First, it places a premium on immediacy of response at the expense of careful consideration. Second, it tends to encourage a crisis orientation in work at the expense of long-term objectives. Third, it means that systematic scrutiny of records goes by default. In addition, of course, it makes impossible the careful preparation which it is suggested lies at the heart of successful supervision. By offering supervision 'on demand', with the implication that the supervisor has ready access to the right answers to particular problems, agencies are denying the complexity of social work intervention. Without preparation, the help the supervisor can give is limited – as will be the value which the worker will accord any such guidance.

In residential work, the opportunities presented by informal supervision are greater. Spontaneous comments made at the time of direct contact with residents can illuminate the worker's understanding of the client's reaction and his own. But formal supervision on the lines discussed here is needed in residential work to provide the opportunity for considered judgements. It is sometimes difficult for staff, who have worked alongside each other handling a resident's crisis, to draw back into a more formal role. Lack of time is then presented as a reason for lack of supervision.

Even where preparation is adequate, the second condition suggested for effective supervision – uninterrupted, regular supervision sessions – is not always satisfied. Again open-plan offices may militate against a free flow of discussion, but even in a private office the telephone may create distraction. Whenever possible, calls should be diverted for the duration of the supervision session. The regularity of the supervision session is important for both supervisor and worker. It provides a framework around which the week can be planned, and it is an explicit statement by the supervisor (and by implication, the agency) of the importance attached to the process.

The third condition – time to make notes and to reflect on the content of supervision – is vital. Not only do the notes of sessions provide a valuable record of the ground covered, what has been achieved, and major issues for future discussion, but they also enable both supervisor and worker to get a longitudinal view of progress when they can refer back to hurdles overcome in the past. Note-taking also represents the importance which the supervisor and the agency attach to supervision – and from this knowledge, the worker can gain in confidence.

Supervisor's responsibilities

After consideration of the agency's responsibilities, it is important to look at those of the supervisor, and at the skills needed to discharge them. Supervision takes place at a number of different levels in the hierarchy of the agency. In order to avoid confusion, the context in which most of the tasks referred to will apply is that of a team leader, senior social worker, or senior probation officer – a supervisor with direct and immediate responsibility for workers whose day-to-day practice brings them into contact with clients. As hierarchies have swollen, other supervisory grades have developed at more senior levels. While the supervision exercised in these posts is closely related to the style of 'enabling' supervision which has been described, it carries a higher proportion of managerial and administrative content. This increases up the hierarchy, so that the Director's relationship with the senior Management Team is one in which supervision, in the sense of instruction and control, has effectively replaced the advice and guidance model. The Director of the agency often has to be assured that a certain course of action will be followed in order to satisfy his own accountability to the public, or employing committee. That assurance can result only if clear instructions are given in the first place.

At team level, the supervisor is expected to fulfil a multiplicity of roles – to allocate work, to organize the work of the team, to set and maintain good standards of practice, to ensure that statutory requirements are fulfilled, to act as a consultant, to advise senior management of the needs of the team and the area, and to communicate and explain management decisions. The multiplicity of roles required is a characteristic of management. The fragmentation of the management task, and a variety of decisions ranging from the trivial to the critical is experienced at all levels, and one of the skills required from the supervisor is to be certain exactly what role is necessary at any one time.

The responsibility of the agency to make space and time for supervision can be subverted by supervisors, who allow other intrusions to distract them from their primary task. The supervisor has to make it clear to the worker that the supervision session assumes priority over other commitments. The time allowed for the session should be laid down in advance. This helps both supervisor and worker to plan their day's work around the session. It is essential to plan the use of time in the session. If it is left entirely to the worker to take the initiative in bringing case material for discussion, the supervisor may fail to get a full picture of the total workload. He may find too that the problems presented by the cases brought for discussion are so numerous that other aspects of work requiring consideration are pushed out by pressure of time. It is suggested therefore that having allocated a fixed duration – ninety minutes is probably the maximum that should be considered for a single session – the supervisor should have in his mind a plan of how this time might be used. While the greater part might go to cases and issues presented by the worker, there should be some kept for a systematic review of the total workload, consideration of new work being undertaken, and discussion of projects or special interests of the worker.

Within this framework, the supervisor has to determine how best to get to know the worker's caseload. Some of the approaches open to the supervisor were discussed in the previous chapter and these could constitute the basis for initial discussion. From a study of case review forms, the priorities of the worker and the particular skills with which he is most confident will become apparent. It is unlikely however that the forms alone will provide sufficient information for discussion. Where there seems to be a lack of fit between the problems presented and the strategy chosen, or where problems are repeated, the supervisor will need to look at the recording of cases by the worker.

Recording

Recording is an important but often overlooked skill in social work. Westheimer comments that 'newly qualified social workers offer no practical evidence that they have been taught in the method of recording' (Westheimer 1977: 149) and a DHSS study found 'agencies seemed to place little emphasis on recording and gave virtually no guidance on the type of recording suitable for different types of cases (Parsloe and Stevenson 1978: 95). Countless typewriter ribbons have been worn out in producing reams of material, which will never be read again – unless something goes wrong. The confusion about the purpose of recording is understandable. Its proper use is as a major component in supervision, so it is worth restating both the *why* and the *how* of recording.

Why record? While many social workers would accept that recording is an integral part of professional development, the reasons given would vary. The trauma of the recent child care tragedies has produced an emphasis on the self-protection which careful recording can offer by demonstrating regular planned contact. This is essentially a negative perception. More positively, records can be used to set down an evolving process of diagnosis and assessment, a plan of intervention, and evaluation of the effectiveness of the plan. The act of committing thoughts to paper forces the worker to clarify and refine his thinking; it gives him a longitudinal picture of the client's social development; and it serves on occasion to spotlight previously over-looked areas which can clarify perception of the client's needs.

How then can these desirable goals best be achieved? The supervisor, who expects high-quality recording, must also ensure that the physical conditions necessary to achieve this goal are available. This means an ample supply of dictation facilities, and the necessary typing support to translate the material on to the file. Without these basic preconditions, it is futile to expect better than the scrappy longhand notes which one sees on case records. But adequate clerical and administrative support is not a justification for the prolix narrative which is sometimes encountered on records. While the amount entered will need to vary according to the nature of the problem, the experience of the worker, and the purpose of the record, a sound guiding principle is to record in a concise manner, stating the objectives of the interview, significant comments or changes in attitude, and any modification necessitated by the interview in the overall plan of intervention.

Recording is a means whereby supervisors can both acquire detailed knowledge of the clients with whom the worker is involved, and make an assessment of the worker's ability. On occasion, particularly with less experienced workers, process recording of an interview could be used to examine closely and carefully the nature of the worker's interaction with clients. As this technique is time consuming, and rightly or wrongly is associated with student status, it is best reserved for situations where the supervisor wishes to demonstrate or reinforce a particular aspect of work. More often the supervisor may use the longitudinal picture offered by the file as the opportunity for a full review of the objectives of continuing social work involvement.

Staff development

From this process the supervisor builds up a picture of the areas where the worker needs to develop. This knowledge is essential before the supervisor can deploy skills in staff development. The skills required in this area are essentially teaching skills. To maximize the contribution from staff development, the supervisor needs to know some basic concepts of adult learning. First, the supervisor must respect the knowledge which the adult learner brings. In social work jargon, this means starting where the worker is. Much will depend on the level of educational attainment. A social worker with a university background, used to tutorial and seminar teaching, will be able to adapt to supervision rapidly, whereas one who left school at sixteen and has had a first career in industry initially may anticipate and *need* a more structured, didactic form of instruction. Similarly, previous experience is likely to govern the readiness of social workers to take notes or to venture possibly mistaken answers. While the supervisor's task is emphatically not that of psychotherapy, he does need to be alert to the influence of previous experiences on present responses.

Second, the motivation of the adult learner is high. Success in a chosen career depends on appropriate attitudes, and more so than most careers social work training emphasizes the need not only for further post-qualifying training but for continuing training throughout a career. Promotion may therefore be linked to further learning. Most basic of all is the desire of the social worker to achieve greater understanding of the clients with whom he works, greater command of social work methods, and thus an enhanced service to those with whom he is working. An important element of supervisory skill is therefore the reinforcement of learning. The supervisor can demonstrate to the worker that new skills or knowledge have been acquired, and help him to integrate, and to apply them.

Third, the integration of managerial responsibility and staff development responsibility may act as a block to students' learning. Some agencies seek to overcome this by splitting the two roles, with staff development responsibilities vesting in a consultant outside the line management structure. The difficulties which this can create are discussed in the next chapter in relation to the problem of leading a team. It is in any event doubtful whether these devices do overcome the basic problem, which is rooted in the reluctance of the worker to expose his failures and inadequacies to the scrutiny of his line manager. Where this reluctance exists, the worker is likely still to suspect that anything which he discloses in supervision may be reported back and used in a negative way. Building up confidence takes time whether the supervisor is also the manager or not.

Consultancy may however have more to offer in residential settings, where the very involvement of supervisor, worker, and client in direct contact may militate against the detached reflection sought from supervision. A consultant, who is not directly involved in the management of an establishment, can enable staff more freely to ventilate their feelings. But in order to ensure the best use of the consultant, it will be necessary clearly to define his role and responsibilities in advance.

How can the supervisor help to build up confidence? He will certainly utilize the high motivation of the adult learner, and will also want to create a favourable climate for learning by seeking to make full use of the worker's previous experiences in a positive way. For instance, the university-trained worker may respond readily to the intellectual challenge of defining goals and objectives whereas the new worker from an industrial background may have superior skills in forming relationships and community mobilization. In each of these cases the supervisor will build from pre-existing strengths by demonstrating to the worker the relevance and importance of what he brings to the job.

It is natural for workers to bring a high degree of anxiety to supervision, especially if they are confronting an unfamiliar situation. Learning to deal with anxiety is a critical task for all social workers, but for managers the task is to contain the anxiety of others as well as to cope with their own anxiety. In this task, the supervisor has a fine balance to maintain between being overly critical and being too accepting of the worker's performance regardless of its quality. The goal is to help the worker to improve his level of work and to grow towards independence in working. Detailed checking of every piece of work can destroy fragile confidence as can ill-considered criticism. The ideal is to create a mutuality of learning in which the worker and supervisor strive together to improve the worker's performance.

The initial response of the supervisor to queries can help to create the climate for this mutual learning. By demonstrating a readiness to give time to discussion – even if the question is naive – by encouraging the worker to question in order to clarify, the supervisor can help in the development of critical examination of situations and of procedures. This process is vital if the worker is to come to function effectively both as a practitioner and as a member of the agency.

In all this the supervisor is trying to achieve a number of objectives. He is offering support at a time of uncertainty, he is encouraging the worker to look critically and objectively at what is being accomplished in his contact with clients, he is helping the worker to find his way through the structure of the agency, and he is assisting the worker to organize his work and his use of time to best advantage. Faced with the demands of a new job, workers sometimes experience difficulty in sorting out priorities for themselves in a way which both satisfies the needs of the agency and offers a reasonable degree of job satisfaction. The period of reflection inherent in supervision does help the worker to think out his priorities and to order his time more effectively.

While individual supervision is the most widely used approach, there are other options open to the manager with overall supervisory responsibility. He can supervise workers in pairs if their needs and experiences are similar. For example, this form of supervision is helpful if workers are engaged on conjoint family therapy or matrimonial work. He can encourage 'twinning' whereby experienced workers afford supervision and case discussion to each other. He can encourage informal 'supervisory' relationships, with an experienced worker taking on responsibility for advice and guidance to a new worker. This will be particularly helpful in residential work where the vagaries of rotas may make it difficult for supervisor and supervisee invariably to be on duty at the same time. This diversification of supervisory patterns can be initially threatening to those used to a rigid hierarchical model, but represents a useful supplement to the professional support available through line management relationships.

Group supervision is in one sense an inevitable aspect of the management role. Characteristically managers operate through the team, and this process is discussed further in Chapter 6. The team leader's role in work allocation and resource provision is considered there, but in relation to staff development the team leader needs to be aware of the potential of group processes to reinforce learning. Pettes (1979) draws attention to the value of 'learning by doing'. Role play, modelling, video, all lend themselves to use in groups and can bring to life an otherwise theoretical discussion.

In residential work, the use of group supervision is essential for it is the ideas, the interactions, and the mutual confidence of the staff group which will be a major determinant of the quality of care afforded to clients. The group has to become the major vehicle for policy-making decisions as well as for the sharing of the stress generated by working with troubled clients.

There is a time-lag between the methodology current in student supervision and its use in staff supervision. Use of video, tape-recordings, and one-way screens which provide supervisors with a direct opportunity to 'observe' the practice of their students has yet to find a place in the repertoire of supervision used in agencies. Supervisors in fieldwork are thus heavily dependent upon what they are told by their staff, and need to find ways in which the veracity of what they are told can be tested. In the absence of 'live' supervision, role play and modelling are two possible methods to improve the accuracy of the supervisor's judgement.

Use of authority

One aspect of authority – the problems which some workers experience as a result of supervision by line managers – has already been discussed. The use of authority by the worker is an area which will present itself in supervision, for in any legal proceedings the worker has to work within the framework of authority vested in him and the agency by the law. Probation officers are described as officers of the court, and among social workers are those most clearly identified with authority and social control functions. This is accepted by most officers, although acute dilemmas are presented when, for example, offenders are placed on probation for possession or smoking of cannabis – an offence which many probation officers would argue should be decriminalized. The most acute conflict has arisen in relation to those charged with political offences such as members of the IRA or Angry Brigade. Here the National Association of Probation Officers has taken a strong line, arguing that probation officers should not be expected to prepare reports in cases where the offender's attitude to the offence, and future prognosis are politically determined rather than a reflection of social and psychological factors. Despite initial hostility from the judiciary to this stand, NAPO's view is now widely accepted. Being an officer of the court need not therefore imply servility. What it does imply and require is clarity about the scope of one's authority, its appropriate use, and its impact on clients.

It is this latter consideration which causes particular anxiety to many social workers. Taught that client self-determination is a cardinal principle of good social work practice, the task of influencing clients to do what the social worker wants is not one that comes easily to practitioners. Yet it may be necessary. A neglectful mother, a disturbed adolescent, or a mentally disordered person may all be the objects of coercive authority – and if they are resistant to the course of action, the social worker will have to deal with the personal conflicts which this exercise of authority creates for him. Often the worker's response will reflect his own experience of authority. The supervisor's task is to help the worker to accept the authority inherent in the role, to talk about and acknowledge the uncomfortable feelings which this sometimes produces, and to assist the natural integration of the worker into the norms of the agency.

The view advanced here is by no means universally shared. Simpkin, amongst others, has pointed to the concealed values of family responsibility, the work ethic, and respect for law and order which underpin social work's functions (Simpkin 1979). Some radical social workers would declare that their role within the superstructure of bureaucratic control is to mobilize their clients, to alert them to the possibilities of collective action, to achieve an awareness within their fellow social workers of the political factors operating on their clients' lives, and to fight for change in the perception of social workers about involvement with trade unions and political movements. Some of those objectives would be shared by liberal reformers too. The divide is between the liberals, who are ready to accept the system and work to change it, and some (though not all) Marxist social workers, in whose view the system is fundamentally corrupted, which means that the worker is justified in subverting it by abusing his position of authority within it.

Helping the worker to accept and use his authority is one aspect of the supervisor's role. Another is his own use of authority in relation to the worker. This may present itself as no more than setting limits to the worker's involvement when his enthusiasm is in danger of leading him into a false position, but more difficulty arises when the very competence of the worker and the validity of his judgements are themselves in question. The supervisor has a dual responsibility, to protect the interests of clients as well as to promote the skill development of the worker. What should be done when the supervisor's perception of a case and the appropriate intervention differs from that of a worker?

The first and most basic assertion is that usually the worker, with his personal knowledge of clients and their needs, will make a more accurate judgement than can the supervisor operating at one remove.

Any supervisor will therefore need to exercise caution and restraint in challenging the views of the worker. If, after discussion and analysis of alternative approaches, there is still a difference of view the supervisor is faced with a decision about whether to allow the worker to pursue his own approach. The factors which should influence that decision are first, whether there is a real risk to the client if the worker's approach fails; second, whether the worker's approach is based on a valid, but different, perception of the client's needs, or is perverse; and third, whether the worker has the capacity to modify his approach if it is not successful.

One of the problems for the supervisor is the prevailing ethos of social work in which there is a reluctance to be firm, and to set clear guidelines. Yet this guidance may be welcomed by insecure students, and should certainly be used where necessary for the protection of clients. The use of supervisory authority may therefore sometimes involve overruling the judgement of the social worker. The occasions on which this is likely to be necessary may be few, but cause much heart-searching because of the potential damage to the confidence and self-image of the worker. When authority is used in this way, it is even more important than usual that the supervisor should make clear his analysis of the clients' needs, the course of action envisaged, and the risks involved so that the worker is clear why a particular decision is being taken.

The exercise of authority may prove necessary in other areas – dress, time-keeping, and social relationships with clients, for example – where fundamentally different attitudes to social work practice may be involved. The uniform of local authority social workers, sweater, beard, and jeans, is a widely held stereotype which like most stereotypes contains elements of both fact and fantasy. The agency setting is a significant influence on dress, as social workers – like all occupational groups – respond to other's expectations. As a generalization, therefore, probation officers and hospital social workers respond to the expectations of the courts and medical colleagues respectively by tending to the conventional in dress. In contrast, social workers based in area offices dress in a more casual fashion. Difficulties may arise when styles appropriate for one setting are transposed to another. For example, an area-based social worker who has to appear in court or a bejeaned hospital social worker may encounter critical comments.

Does this peripheral issue matter? Is it not what a worker says or does that matters, not what he wears? In an ideal world society should make its judgements on the basis of actions and not appearance, but in reality the physical impression which is given by the appearance of a worker does influence perception. In the examples given deviance from the norm of the setting will not only attract criticism for the worker but also influence the weight which is given to his views. In some settings therefore compliance with minimum standards of dress may be in the client's interests. The worker who insists on his personal freedom of choice may do so at the risk of impairing the opportunities for his client. Where this arises the supervisor may need to use his authority by insisting on compliance with accepted standards.

Social workers enjoy a generally relaxed attitude to time-keeping compared with most office-based workers. In recognition of the necessity of evening work, it is expected that social workers will take time off in office hours. An increasing number of local authorities are adopting flexi-time schemes whereby social workers record their hours worked. While there are problems in relation to a strict flexi-time system, as core content rarely covers the time when social workers pay home visits, it does offer considerable advantages to social workers. The difficulty may be in readjusting the workload in order to take time off, but flexi-time does give managers a prescribed working week with which to plan systems of workload management.

Managers are more likely to experience problems where no system exists for recording starting and finishing times. It is difficult to monitor the time actually worked by social workers. Home visits provide the perfect alibi for the delinquent social worker. Most offices have a story, which has passed into folk wisdom, of a social worker who, saying that he was off to do home visits, instead disappeared to the races or his girlfriend. How then can managers exercise some control over standards of time-keeping? While the 'disappearing' social worker may not be evident in all offices, problems with unreliable time-keeping may arise more frequently with workers turning up late for court or being absent when their office duty comes around.

The nature of social work practice is such that workers will operate at different levels and work at different paces. One worker may achieve in a couple of hours' contact changes which would take another worker several weeks or even months of contact to achieve.

But the problems being discussed here are not those of the rapid worker, who meets the requirements of the agency satisfactorily and then goes home to dig the garden. In this situation, the interests of neither clients nor colleagues are jeopardized. When, however, a careless attitude to the discipline of keeping appointments and meeting commitments imposes a greater burden on others it is appropriate for the manager to intervene. It is sometimes tempting to refrain from action when colleagues appear to cover absences without demur. In the long run such restraint is more likely to be viewed as a sign of weakness. Initial irritation about defective time-keeping can fester with its constant repetition until it becomes a disruptive influence on office relationships. Better by far to express concern to the worker and make clear the expectations of the agency and of the manager. If this has no impact the manager may need to make explicit the possible consequences of continued poor time-keeping – and if no change results after these warnings, disciplinary action needs consideration. That raises broader issues which are considered below.

The third area where authority may be used by managers is in the context of social relationships with clients. Here the climate is far more relaxed than was the case when preoccupation with quasi-clinical modes of practice meant that emotional involvement of worker with client was viewed as indicative of bad practice. Now a more normal attitude is accepted with the emphasis rightly on the worker's ability to control his feelings and retain objectivity about the needs of his clients. The formality of office interviews and sometimes sterile home visits is supplemented by informal meetings with clients in pubs and clubs. Without wishing to resuscitate the old prohibitions, the manager needs to recognize that this is treacherous ground. It is all too easy for the worker to be trapped into a wholly social conversation rather than purposeful contact. It is also easy for the client to deny the reality underlying the contact. The worker who chooses to operate in this informal way needs to be very clear and explicit – to manager and to client – about his role and its limitations if misunderstandings are to be avoided.

Inevitably sometimes the boundaries will become blurred. Sometimes too the worker may be involved in a relationship which becomes far deeper than a professional one. Such a situation demands exceptionally sensitive handling if the reputation of worker and agency are to be unscathed and no harm caused to the client. The inquiry into the

Paul Brown case in the Wirral was told of unsubstantiated rumours, subsequently established to be false, that one of the social workers was having an affair. Rumour and innuendo were rife. Social workers are in a position of trust where the community expects them to care for the vulnerable and to protect them. Any relationship which exploits vulnerability, rather than protecting it, needs to be dealt with severely. Unhappily for managers, such black and white examples are rare. Only by reference to the particular circumstances can a judgement be made, but with their threefold responsibility to worker, client, and agency supervisors need to be alive to both the private and public consequences of action and inaction. But just as social workers faced with difficult decisions may rarely find their problems eased by delay, so too supervisors need to guard against a Micawberish hope that something will turn up to resolve the problem.

Evaluation

The nature of supervisory responsibilities has changed with the expansion both in terms of volume and complexity that has characterized the personal social services. The friendly informal relationships which had rested as much on personal respect as on formal status have been replaced by more explicit managerial tasks. One of the first examples of the shift occurred in the context of the probation and after-care service. The Butterworth Report in 1972 introduced a division between 'A' and 'B' grade workers. Despite the inversion of normal parlance in that 'B' grade offered both status and enhanced salary, this proposal was bitterly divisive. Its impact in probation was all the greater because, as has been said, the service emphasized the individual officer as the key figure in delivering a service to clients more than most social work settings.

Butterworth recommended that 'B' grade would be open to 'competent and dedicated' main grade probation officers after a minimum of three years' service. Probation committees determined different procedures and policies for implementation of this recommendation, and in some areas only half those eligible were given 'B' grade. An annual evaluation was the means whereby recommendations were prepared for the probation committee, and thus the senior probation officers found themselves with effective control over the salary grading and status of their staff. 'A' and 'B' gradings were never popular.

NAPO launched a campaign to achieve a unified salary scale, and eventually succeeded. Ironically the probation service abandoned its division of the basic grade at about the same time as the national framework of three levels of social worker emerged in the wake of the social workers' strike. Thus first-line managers in social services departments found themselves needing to evaluate their staff, knowing that their evaluation might have a direct impact on grading.

The anxiety that is expected of students on placement, or workers in their probationary months, is carried over to more experienced workers if gradings and salary levels are dependent on the outcome of evaluation. The defence mechanisms produced by anxiety – regression, projection, and denial – should be anticipated by the supervisor. Thus some workers will deal with the stress created by evaluation by regressing to a situation with which they feel comfortable, for instance reducing the number of child abuse cases and seeking to increase the proportion of their work related to services. Others will project responsibility for any weaknesses in their performance on to others – the inadequacy of clerical support being held to blame for poor recording, the low quality of supervision received being held responsible for lack of insight, or unrealistic demands of management being blamed for failure to complete a piece of work on time. And others may deal with their anxiety by denial, by refusing to acknowledge that particular instructions or guidance were issued, or by failing to communicate.

By the time a formal evaluation is undertaken, the supervisor should be familiar both with the worker's abilities and with his workload responsibilities. There should therefore be nothing in the evaluation that has not previously been discussed with the worker – a further reason for regular supervision for all workers. One of the saddest instances in the introduction of 'A' and 'B' grading in the probation service was the decision to give only 'A' grade to an officer of sixty-four who had joined the service as a single-handed worker over forty years earlier, who had become an institution in the area, but who had never been effectively supervised. To him, the rejection which 'A' grade implied was a bitter blow which soured his memory of a lifetime's work. Supervision might not have greatly improved his level of performance, but it would have prepared him for a judgement of his work, and better equipped him for the outcome of his evaluation.

The worker should know when the evaluation is to take place, and the areas to be covered in the evaluation. While it can be useful for the supervisor occasionally to back a hunch in discussion of the work undertaken, it is essential that a formal evaluation should be based on evidence. If an appeal is lodged – and most authorities provide for this, at least where decisions about grading are involved – the supervisor will have to substantiate his judgements. But if the evaluation is about grading, the supervisor is not only making a judgement about the capacity of the worker but also comparing the worker's level of performance with a standard – of a level one, level two or level three worker. Although the national framework and local agreements may prescribe in general terms the expectations held in relation to a particular grade, it is still for the supervisor to determine whether that standard has been reached. It is rare to find departments which set explicit criteria, but without criteria the supervisor is forced to rely on his own experience and values to a degree which can lead to inconsistencies with other areas where the supervisors have different experiences.

One way of minimizing this problem is to ensure that supervisors meet together, ideally in an agency workshop, to thrash out a common approach and a common standard. By discussing problems and identifying the criteria to be applied, it should be possible for the group to minimize the disparities in application of any evaluation scheme. There are core areas for any evaluation of competence which the supervisor will need to weigh in regard to both the local agreement and the common criteria agreed with colleagues.

An evaluation needs to include material which will enable management to assess the worker's knowledge, his skills, his written work, his management of his own workload, his use of supervision, and his operation as a member of a group of workers with common goals. Many of these points have been referred to elsewhere in this chapter.

Knowledge: This section covers the knowledge of legislative provision and statutory requirements relevant to the worker's area of functioning. But it goes further than mere possession of the knowledge for it also relates to the use of knowledge. A worker who never remembers the fine points of wardship proceedings but knows when to seek advice can thus satisfy the requirements of this heading. But the worker who neither knows the law nor sees its relevance will be evaluated critically. The law is only one aspect, for this heading can also cover the community resources available in the locality and knowledge of the functions and powers of other agencies.

Skills: This covers the area of casework practice, including the ability to establish and use relationships with clients, and the formulation of realistic objectives. The ability to use authority appropriately, to make accurate assessments of situations, and to maintain a sense of purpose in one's work are aspects that come within this heading. It is related to but different from the next heading.

Workload management: The deployment of skills is only effective when allied to planned use of time. Social work time is a limited resource, and the worker has to be able to use his time to best advantage. That means selecting priorities, establishing objectives, and reconciling the many demands on time in a way that gives a good service to the agency while preserving the worker's sanity. Making time for agency meetings, for group projects, and for recording are other facets which indicate that the worker is able to accommodate potentially conflicting demands. In social work, the best-laid plans are vulnerable to change as emergencies distort timetables – a case conference, a mental health section, or a family crisis can occupy several hours in a week yet cannot be planned in advance. The ability to cope with that pressure is an important part of any evaluation.

Recording: Written work is the part of a worker's performance most open to scrutiny, and where feedback may be available from other agencies. The standard of reports and letters is open to more objective judgement than many areas of practice. The standard of recording too can be evaluated, not in terms of its literary qualities, but the feel which it gives of the worker's understanding of the client. Most workers fall behind with recording at some stage in their career. When this happens, the subsequent recording is of limited utility for it lacks the immediacy of perception possible when the record is prepared a day or two after the interview.

Use of supervision: The worker's ability to use supervision is appropriate for consideration in an evaluation, for it is this which will demonstrate a capacity for development. Factors for consideration under this heading will include the capacity for reflection and the use of discussion to clarify and (where necessary) to modify the initial views held.

Membership of a team: In any agency, the worker will not be operating in isolation. Even the probation officer working single-handed in a rural area, or a social worker working with other professionals in a hospital, will have a reference group of their colleagues even if they meet less frequently than would be the case in an urban area office. In each case the worker's ability to contribute his experience to the group will be relevant to evaluation. The team too may operate as in the hospital context as a multi-disciplinary team. The ability to co-operate with other agencies and other disciplines as well as with social work colleagues will therefore be tested.

If the supervisor considers these aspects of performance, he should be able to complete a reasonably comprehensive evaluation which matches the worker's attainment against that expected for the grade, taking into account the worker's experience. Although evaluation in this context is primarily used as a management document, the supervisor can and should use it as a focus for further discussion in supervision. Any areas of weakness identified in the written document should be worked at with learning tasks being mutually defined. The act of putting in writing even previously acknowledged areas of weakness can be very threatening to the worker. If it is accompanied by a plan agreed in supervision for remedying the weakness, prefer-ably formulated in a way which enables the worker to measure progress, some of the anxiety experienced may be mitigated.

Formulating learning objectives is not easy. The concept is bor-rowed from training courses for the Certificate in Social Services. It describes the process of setting objectives for a course of training which can be expressed in behavioural terms. As such the achieve-ment or otherwise of the objectives is susceptible to measurement. Now this approach is very different to the usual approach adapted by social workers towards training. This defines training in terms of the acquisition and assimilation of knowledge, or in terms of personal growth and development. There is a place in social work for personal development but it should be related to the tasks of the worker in question. It should be the result of his acquisition of job-related skills, not an end in itself.

A course in family therapy will – on the basis of the approach – be appropriate provided that the worker has clients for whom such techniques would be helpful, and provided that the worker has the time to devote to develop new approaches.

Learning objectives might then be defined in relation to an in-creased use of family therapy techniques with a greater number of clients. A course in wardship legislation might have as its learning objective reduced dependence of the worker on consultation on the legal framework, or a course on work with alcoholics might mean learning objectives for the worker of a higher incidence of alcoholics on his caseload, use of his knowledge and skills as a resource for other team members, and assumption of a liaison role with a local clinic. It is by the translation of overall objectives into highly specific goals that the worker can be helped to grow in confidence as he gradually sees progress.

Supervision in residential settings

The difficulties inherent in supervision of residential practice have been touched upon above. The benefits of actuality and immediacy have to be set against the liabilities of pressure, stress, and involvement which militate against detachment. A further problem is the frequent lack of clarity about supervisory responsibility due to the complexity of rota systems, and the often ambiguous role of managers and advisers in residential care who do not work in an establishment but exercise an overall advisory and monitoring responsibility.

Where responsibility for supervision is diffuse, it is critical that all those involved spend time in sorting out an approach to supervision. Some of the options open to managers were identified above in terms of pairing and informal linkages. But these roles have to be made explicit if subsequent confusion is to be avoided. There may be utility in a formal *contract* which sets down the supervisors, their roles, the nature of supervisory contact, and any record to be kept while also clarifying the expectations of the worker's performance.

The focus of much of this chapter has been on the individual worker and supervisor, but the staff development role of managers has to go beyond the micro-involvement with individuals to the team and area. The next chapter considers techniques of developing teamwork, which while not formally labelled supervision require many of the skills used in individual work.

5

Leading a team

The importance of teams as the means whereby social work – and social services – are delivered has grown throughout the years since the Local Authority Social Services Act (1970). A number of factors have influenced this development. First, the range of specialisms drawn together in the social services department was such that no single practitioner could be expected to encompass them all with equal competence. Whereas previously members of small departments offering a single service had shared a common knowledge base, now child care officers had to grapple with mental health legislation, and those formerly responsible for the mentally ill found themselves responsible for the care of the elderly in the community. A sense of interdependence was the immediate result. Second, the emphasis in the Seebohm Report on the community and the development of area-based teams working to develop community resources prompted an examination of the responsibilities of the group as a whole to meet the needs of the area. The individual orientation of casework was supplemented by a focus on group and community work. Third, the explosion of referrals forced departments to look at the differentiation of the fieldwork task with the employment of social work assistants to take on the more routine work dealing with review visiting of the elderly, minor aids, and practical assistance. Fourth, despite the hierarchical structure of local government reproduced in social services departments there was a strong participative sense in departments fostered by mutual involvement in a new venture and by the prevailing ethos of social work, favouring group involvement and sharing.

The combination of these influences meant that social services departments looked to teams as the basic unit for the administration and delivery of fieldwork services. In other agencies, and in particular the probation and after-care service, teamwork's development can be traced to rather different origins. It was strongly influenced by what was happening in social services departments, but also reflected the impact of conjoint working. The probation and after-care service had long experience of workers operating in pairs with a matrimonial case, a different worker relating to each partner, and now began to apply the team concept to other groups of clients. Thus one worker might develop particular expertise in employment finding, another particular skills in psychosexual problems, and another in family therapy. The needs of a client might thus require contact with more than one member of the team, but the net result was an amplification of the skills used in the client's service. This latter approach resembles the community team in the typology discussed below which draws on that developed by Payne (1979).

Traditional team

Before 1970, the usual organizational pattern was that of a team led by a senior social worker and consisting of a group of staff with equal status working independently except for the supervision which they received. Other services offered by the agency – residential, domiciliary, or day care – were usually organized completely separately. This model of the *traditional team* may still be found, although rarely in social services departments where the use of other skills and the links with other forms of service delivery have created a more differentiated pattern. Some probation offices and voluntary agencies continue to operate on this basis. It is structured to encourage, almost to require, individual casework rather than community involvement. Its strength however is that all members of the team are clear about their roles and responsibilities, procedures for the involvement of other services or agencies are clearly defined, and for new workers the freedom to make one's own mistakes albeit with supportive supervision is often helpful.

Transitional team

The transitional team is one in which ancillary staff are clearly recognized as part of the team, close relationships (often including shared responsibility for clients) are developed with other welfare services, and work is shared on the basis of allocation to the worker whose expertise best matches the need of the clients. This evolution happened swiftly in social services departments. The myth of the multi-purpose social worker coping with all referrals was quickly exposed.

The high incidence of work with the elderly and handicapped demanded different skills from the worker. There was a greater emphasis on assessment for services, and a wide knowledge of available resources was of greater utility than skilled social casework.

The bath aid became a symbol of misuse of social work skills as CQSW holders found themselves supplying aids rather than applying what they had learned on their training courses. The number of cases closed on the day of referral, or within the first month of contact, demanded a radically different style of work from the extended casework model which remained the primary method taught on social work courses.

Home helps, occupational therapists, adaptations technicians, and community workers are fully integrated in teams operating this model. Allocation procedures reflect the different skills of staff. Developing this approach to define the specifically social work task became the dominant preoccupation of the profession. The DHSS report on Manpower and Training for the Social Services (Birch Report 1976) had attempted to identify the tasks which a CQSW holder should be expected to fulfil. A BASW working party report in 1977 (BASW 1977) produced an important, albeit much criticized statement which sought to identify work which should be the exclusive prerogative of the social worker. The Barclay Inquiry into social work had the lack of a clear definition of social work as its framework, and was asked to clarify the roles and responsibilities of the profession.

The transitional team has then one huge liability – it creates role confusion. But does this matter in terms of the service which clients receive? The flexibility in using staff often led to an amplification of the service received. True, the cherished Seebohm concept of one worker per family can scarcely be reconciled with this approach in which the re-emergence of specialist skills is implicit. But being able to utilize the occupational therapist for advice on aids to daily living, the home help for practical assistance, and the social work assistant for routine visiting, does enormously strengthen the social worker's professional role by enabling him to concentrate on his primary task.

Community team

The community team is the third point on the continuum in Payne's analysis. He describes it as a more complex mechanism in which 'social workers are involved in a network which can be described as part of the community support system' (Payne 1979: 151). Roles within the team are merged with much informal sharing of responsibility for work. Para-professionals are accepted as integral members of the team. There is much emphasis on working with the community and developing responses at a community level rather in terms of individual pathology.

While Payne sees these three teams as part of a continuum, it is questionable whether the fully fledged community team which he describes is a logical development from the transitional team. The latter offers a degree of flexibility in use of staff which to many managers will prove attractive without abandoning the concept of prescribed worker–client responsibilities, which may be the end product of the community team. How far teams move is not a matter for the manager alone. Brill, one of the most influential writers on the evolution of teamwork, charts four stages in the evolution of teams which managers need to recognize if they are successfully to handle a tense and stressful period (Brill 1976).

The initial stage of *orientation* is one in which members of a team find out about the strengths and weaknesses of themselves and their colleagues as a necessary precursor of *accommodation*, the process of modifying an individual's tasks, attitudes, or relationship in order to make the team overall operate more effectively. *Negotiation* follows as the bargaining process about boundaries develops (very much characteristic of the transitonal team in the typology adopted above), and interdependent relationships develop. Finally *operation* as members work together, readily accepting interdependence and shared responsibility but with the team as a protective shield and strength for all its members. This conceptual analysis can be applied to most group situations. It can be of assistance to hesitant team leaders to have this framework available. When the going gets tough, it is often worthwhile to take a step back to think out the various stages of the team development process.

What is here described is the process by which a team evolves in its thinking. But in addition to the process, the team leader will need to be alert to both formal and informal relationships within the group. Sometimes, for instance, while formal responsibility for aspects of child care practice may be vested in a senior social worker, the team may operate by identifying another worker as an unofficial consultant in this area to whose opinion others defer. It is as important for managers to be aware of these informal networks as of the strengths and weaknesses of individuals in the team when work is being allocated.

Allocation

Allocation is a highly emotive area of work, yet it has become so only in the years since social services departments came into being. All generalizations are dangerous, including this one, but most agencies operated a variant of the patch system in pre-Seebohm Report days. This meant simply that each worker was responsible for all the work coming from a particular geographical area. This might be subject to modification if a worker was overloaded, a case presented special difficulties, or another worker had previous contact, but broadly speaking it operated in most local authorities. In urban areas with a heavy load of office duty work, the system was modified to facilitate a fair distribution of that work.

A few authorities continue to operate on this basis, and as patch-work (which will be discussed more fully in the next chapter) has again become fashionable the virtues of this traditional allocation method are again being recognized. It is simple. It is clear. It enables the worker to know and become known by the community where he operates. Simplicity and clarity are underrated virtues and highly complex and time-consuming procedures have been more character-istic of local authorities.

Why did the simple model fail to meet the needs of the enlarged departments? Essentially it was unable to provide for the complexity of need, demanding different skills and different workers, and the volume of need, aptly expressed in the term 'bombardment' which is used to describe the task of coping with referrals. As a consequence, initially in urban areas but subsequently very widely adopted nationally, one saw the development of intake teams. These offered a neat organizational solution: a group of workers taking primary responsibility for all new referrals and working with them until it became clear that transfer to a long-term team was necessary. The implications of both patch and intake organizational models are of vital importance, and lie at the heart of the current enquiry into social work. In different ways however they limit the problem of allocation, one by determining the worker on the basis of geography, the other by the nature of referral and the anticipated timescale of intervention.

If a patch system is not in force, the team leader has responsibility for allocation. The way in which he discharges this task will influence the development of the team. Direct allocation of work, like the patch model, has the virtue of simplicity. It is based on the presumption that the team leader knows the strengths and weaknesses of each worker, and the space available in their workload for additional work. In this regard it is closely aligned to the practice of workload management discussed in Chapter 3. Whatever system of allocation is adopted, the team leader has a residual responsibility to ensure an equitable distribution of work between team members. This responsibility is most acute in a system of direct allocation, where accusations of unfairness and bias can poison the atmosphere if any grounds exist for discontent. The weaknesses of direct allocation are threefold. First, it means that individual workers often have little awareness of the overall position of the team and its workload. Second, it militates against the development of team spirit and a sense of collective identity. And third, it places a heavy premium on the knowledge of the team leader and his sensitivity to the pressures on the team.

Perhaps the most commonly found model, and also the most controversial, is that of group allocation through the medium of the team meeting. This involves the whole team in the decision-making process. All referrals received in the preceding week are summarized in the group meeting, discussed, and then a team member may – or may not – offer to take on the work. The benefits of this approach are the converse of the weaknesses of direct allocation. It gives each worker a clear picture of the total demands on the team and an awareness of the pressure being experienced by colleagues. It promotes a strong sense of team identity and enables the team as a unit to work at finding solutions to problems facing the team in coping with the flow of work. And it enables the team leader to share the onerous burden of securing fair allocation of work.

Yet group allocation is open to many objections. The pragmatic managerial objection to the process relates to the time it takes. In the not atypical example described below, the time involved amounted to three hours each week for each team leader, and one to one and a half hours for each social worker, occupational therapist, and social work assistant – a substantial slice of working time equivalent in total to a complete working week for one social worker. But in addition to the time involved in this process, allocation meetings tend to become overlaid by considerable complexity, involving administrative staff as well as fieldworkers.

There are rarely two identical systems of allocation. That described here offers an illustration of a highly developed and quite sophisticated process. On the day before the allocation meeting, the team leaders in the area meet to consider a tray piled high with the week's referrals. Already some filtering will have taken place. The intake senior has four choices in relation to each referral: to close the case (and Goldberg and Warburton's work (1979) indicated a high proportion of same-day closures), to pend awaiting further information, to work with the case in the duty system with a view to subsequent allocation or closure, or to bring the work forward for allocation. The team leaders then review the cases, determining the category of worker which should be involved with particular problems. Sometimes this decision is relatively easy – a child abuse case will usually require social work skills, a request for a major adaptation those of an occupational therapist – but often a degree of joint working will be indicated. In addition, the team leaders use a complex scoring system to determine priorities for allocation of those cases considered. By the time of the allocation meeting, the team leaders then know the work to be allocated, and have agreed their priorities.

The allocation meeting consists of social workers and occupational therapists. In many areas social work assistants are also present. The intake senior describes the week's referrals, often reading direct from the referral form. Occasionally questions seeking clarification will be asked. Referrals outstanding from previous weeks will also be presented. Each client has a score based on the system referred to above, which provides a rudimentary assessment of the urgency of needs presented. After describing each case, the intake senior invites offers. The response to this invitation will depend on the volume of work currently carried by the team at the time, and the overall morale of the team. While team leaders will often know through explicit workload management or through supervision when workers have space to take additional clients, they will not utilize this knowledge in group allocation, relying instead on tacit group pressure. Cases which remain unallocated are brought forward the following week with a higher priority ranking, in order to ensure allocation.

Reservations about group allocation techniques do go further than the time involved. As one of the respondents to the DHSS study conducted by Parsloe and Stevenson commented 'The allocation meeting allegedly allows a democratic choice. In reality it works out that the less strong minded get lumbered' (Parsloe and Stevenson 1978: 73). The role of the team leader is as critical in group allocation as in direct allocation. While his explicit power is circumscribed, in practice his influence is paramount both in relation to the presentation of information about clients referred and in the pressure which he puts upon the team to take work.

Whatever method of allocation is adopted will influence the team's attitude to its leader. Whether this is positive or negative will depend on the previous experiences of the team. There is no right way in which to allocate work, but intriguingly the DHSS survey found that most workers were well satisfied with the procedure used in their team to the extent of rejecting any alternative. But the role of the team leader is also seen as a critical influence on the provision of resources, on relationships with senior management, and on the way in which team meetings are used.

Use of time

The major social work resource is that of time – professional time. Yet surveys have repeatedly shown that only 25–30 per cent of the average social worker's week is spent in direct contact with clients. It is of course simplistic to argue that if this proportion could be increased by a concomitant decrease in time-consuming bureaucratic procedures or reducing the number of meetings, all would be well. Social work activities extend more widely than direct contact with clients. Advocacy with the DHSS on behalf of a client, attempts to mobilize community resources, and efforts to change environmental pressures are extremely time-consuming but often highly significant in clients' lives. Nevertheless time available for work with or on behalf of clients will be a preoccupation of the team leader. Working groups, team projects, allocation meetings, and study discussions are all important in different ways but they are subordinate to the primary objective of a social work team – to offer an effective service to clients. Managing time to reconcile team effectiveness with the flair and initiative that participatory work can generate is thus essential.

Accommodation

But in addition to the use of time, the manager will be concerned with the impact of physical resources upon the team. The responsibilities of management in this area were clearly described in the report of the Paul Brown Inquiry. There was not much comfort for social workers in many of the inquiry reports on child care, but on the issue of physical resources the Brown Report was explicit. 'Adequate accommodation is the necessary tool of the social worker just as machinery is for the factory worker.' It went on:

> 'the long-term aim should be purpose-built offices with plenty of sound-proof interview rooms; play areas and creches where children can be kept while their parents are being interviewed; comfortable suitable waiting areas for the old, handicapped and mothers with children; entrances and passages suitable for the infirm; and offices which are quiet, private and pleasant enough to enable the staff to make thoughtful judgements in often harrowing cases.'

(Brown Report 1980: 19)

While the last clause has to be an expression of hope, the description of office accommodation fairly conveys what area offices and probation offices need.

Having described the ideal, the report goes on tellingly to describe the actual accommodation of the social workers. One office had restricted access for the disabled, an inadequate waiting area, and needed a coat of paint. Another sited area teams 'in a warren of offices thinly partitioned off from each other. We saw peeling paint, chipped plaster, evidence of damp and bare floorboards covered with odd scraps of carpet' (Brown Report 1980: 20). In a third,

> 'we heard evidence of continuing problems with damp and with the wiring, plumbing, heating and security of the building . . . we saw for ourselves the trailing cables, holes in the floor, chunks of plaster missing from the walls and the evidence of damp. We heard of infestations of woodlice, outcrops of fungus, and the persistence of unexplained unpleasant smells.'   (Brown Report 1980: 20)

And similar conditions prevailed elswhere. The report concludes that 'the inadequate office facilities . . . exacerbated the problems of work of the staff' (Brown Report 1980: 25).

The response of management in this sorry situation has to be unequivocal. A decent professional job cannot be done in squalid overcrowded conditions when privacy, quiet reflection, and uninterrupted supervision are essential components in good practice. Managers therefore have a responsibility unremittingly to draw the attention of both senior management and elected members to the inadequacies of their accommodation, and to press for improvements. That is the limit of their managerial responsibility but in some situations where continued pressure has failed to elicit a response they will have a responsibility as professionals and/or as trade unionists to take further action in support of their representations. The quality of social work agencies' office accommodation says much about the way in which society as a whole, and employing agencies in particular, perceive social work's clientele. This perception has to be challenged at all levels of agency management.

The middle manager

If a team leader is critical of senior management, he does undeniably run the risk of alienating those further up the managerial hierarchy. Whatever their position senior managers are no different from anybody else. They prefer to be praised rather than criticized, and they prefer to be liked rather than disliked, although the unpleasant phenomenon of the 'macho manager' determined to prove that he's the meanest son of a bitch in the department is increasingly visible. Yet there is within social work agencies a greater capacity for accepting criticism than will be found in most hierarchical settings.

The shared professional identity of social workers does not however wholly undermine local government values which assert the primacy of the Chief Officer. The middle manager then has an unenviable position as marginal man in the structure. He is daily exposed to the stress, tensions, and frustrations of his staff but has no power to alter the resources available or departmental policy. And he has to interpret managerial decisions, from which he may dissent personally, to his team and secure their compliance.

How can this delicate balance best be struck? It is evident that skills in communication – both written and oral – are of paramount importance for the marginal man. He has to be able to convey to management the needs of his team in terms of physical resources, he has to ensure that the needs of the community in the area are fully represented to those responsible for planning and resource allocation, and he has to participate with colleagues from other areas in discussions to ensure that policies are applied consistently and fairly throughout the department. No one individual has the knowledge to fulfil these various roles without help. The middle manager will have to use his team's resources and knowledge to make him fully effective, and to do so has to communicate to the team the rationale for and relevance of communicating information upwards. When he does so, he is entitled to expect response. Nothing is more depressing for team morale than substantial effort on a piece of work, which, after it is communicated to senior management, disappears into a void never to emerge again in any recognizable form. The free flow of minutes of management meetings at all levels is the minimum requirement to avoid this vacuum.

The transmission of information from management to fieldworkers offers infinite possibilities for miscommunication. It is natural for those at the bottom of a hierarchical structure to feel suspicious of the intentions of those at the top. Failures of resources, policy decisions restricting freedom of action, political decisions conveyed by management to staff are all seen as the direct responsibility of management and its wilful refusal to hear unpalatable messages. Some suspicion then is endemic. The task of management is to minimize alienation. The best way to achieve this goal is to create an open structure in which information passes freely up and down the hierarchy. At present information flows upwards very much more freely than it does downwards (Streatfield and Wilson 1980). Wide circulation of minutes of departmental meetings, an agency news bulletin, and in large far-flung departments a formal staff consultative council, are ways in which such a structure can be facilitated. Fantasy can be handled where information is readily available – it flourishes on rumour and half-truths. At team level, the team leader should try to make time for discussion of new policies and to ensure that not only managerial decisions but also the background to them are fully presented to the team.

Using team resources

Team meetings are the obvious medium for discussion of this kind, but they serve many other functions. While the amount of time which social workers spend in meetings has assumed the status of popular mythology, that spent with fellow members of the team will usually be worthwhile in promoting an open structure, a sense of sharing, and a willingness to contribute individual skills and talents to a wider group. In the open structure advocated, considerable time will be taken in feeding up to senior management the concerns of the team, ways in which it would wish to see changes in policy or views on resource allocation priorities. There is often a ferment of ideas and much experimentation taking place at team level which is not communicated, perhaps for fear that 'they' will want to control or influence the pattern of experiment. Yet if these ideas are not passed on, the latent gap between practitioners and managers can swiftly become unbridgeable.

Projects are very popular in primary schools. They enable children to explore different aspects of a subject. They help children to learn how best to work together and share in a common task. They stimulate interest by making a break from routine. Used sparingly projects can achieve each of these objectives in a social work setting. They need to be used sparingly because of the demands which they undoubtedly make on the time of the participants, but if well chosen they can add much to the life and vigour of the team. Two examples will suffice. A social worker moved from an area operating a patch-based system of work allocation to one organized on an intake and long-term team basis. Holding strong views about the merits of patch, he could have launched a frontal assault to secure a change in the basis of work. He would probably have failed at the cost of alienating his colleagues. Instead he suggested that as a team project a resource map should be prepared logging all community resources in a particular area – GPs, clergy, community nursing, voluntary organizations, volunteers, etc. The exercise achieved two goals. It gave the team a sense of unity. It also showed them how little they actually knew of what was available in the community, and how little use was made of existing resources. The moral was understood. The social worker won assent to a modified experiment with a patch system.

The other example from the probation service is a familiar one of the team recognizing a common problem – the high incidence of unemployment among offenders in the 17–21 age range – and attempting to tackle it by organizing a programme of social skills training. Although the initiative stemmed from two officers who ran the group, the whole team became engaged in the project by providing back-up when one of the officers was absent. The senior was able to use the group to demonstrate to some of the more traditionalist officers, geared to office reporting, that other approaches could be beneficial. By referring their own clients to the group, officers were able to explore the potential of collaborative teamwork and its capacity to enhance what could be offered in the individual officer–client relationship.

Using a project as an indirect means of developing teaching is a reminder of the important role of the team leader in developing staff skills. When a sense of unity has been created, role play can provide a helpful way to reinforce teaching. The Open University has a teaching pack on child abuse which contains a simulated case conference. This can be used at a number of different levels – in multi-disciplinary training courses as a means of helping professionals to a better understanding of each other's role and responsibilities, in social work training as a means of helping social workers to be assertive in a difficult and stressful setting, and in departments as a means of focusing on the skills needed to chair case conferences. Allied to video, which gives an opportunity for participants to witness the group interactions, role play can bring life and interest to team-training activities.

A further aspect of using team meetings in this way is securing feedback from training courses. Too often considerable resources are devoted to sending staff on courses to pursue a special interest or acquire new skills, but on their return to the team little interest is displayed in the course and its potential benefit to the individual and the team is dissipated. By providing a formal opportunity for feedback, the team leader can demonstrate the value accorded to training as well as helping the individual to integrate and use his newly acquired knowledge. The length of time given to this activity will obviously be varied to reflect the nature of the courses undertaken. It can sometimes be linked to the presentation of case material for discussion purposes with practical illustrations of how particular techniques can be helpful. Unlike medicine and the law, social work training provides little opportunity for 'sitting with Nelly' and learning from observation of practice. Yet there is a great value in providing this experience and team meetings through role play and discussions can be of inestimable benefit to both long-serving and inexperienced workers.

Advisers and consultants

This chapter hitherto has been based on the assumption that the team leader has dual responsibility for the organization of the team and allocation of work on the one hand, and for the quality of professional practice on the other. That is the most usual organizational pattern encountered in social work agencies. It is not however the only one. The most popular alternative model is to use a consultant for the professional practice and staff development role. Consultation, like supervision and accountability, is one of those words frequently used in social work circles to lend authority to remarks, but which on closer study turns out to have a number of differing, or sometimes mutually exclusive, meanings. Before discussing the possible contribution of consultants it is therefore necessary to define the term.

To begin with a negative – consultation is not supervision. The relationship between a team leader and his staff is supervisory. Sometimes casework consultation is offered in the mistaken belief that the use of this term will lead social workers to overlook the reality of the managerial relationship. The unvarnished truth is that consultation can only be given by one outside the line management role, but who uses his skill and expertise to advise and assist the social worker better to understand the particular problems presented by the client. Consultation, as in a medical context, presupposes that the recipient is free to accept or reject the advice proferred. As such it is usually reserved for the more experienced members of staff, or those in supervisory posts, who are presumed to exercise a high degree of professional automony in their daily functions.

Where a consultant is used in relation to practice, the relationship between the line manager and the consultant needs careful exploration between the parties to the contact. If consultation is offered in line with the definition above, the lines are relatively clear. The consultant is a resource for the practitioner, but formal responsibility for work undertaken rests with the worker and his line manager. The contact and feedback from consultant to line manager needs to be negotiated and formally recorded so that the social worker knows exactly what can be expected to pass from one to the other.

The situation becomes less clear when the consultant is given formal responsibility for the quality of practice. This division between the organizational responsibility of the team leader and practice responsibility of the consultant proceeds from the assumption that the span of control and range of skills demanded of the team leader make it unrealistic to expect one person to encompass them all. Better by far, runs the argument, to have defined areas of responsibility to which the skills of supervisory staff can be matched. This concept has a superficial attraction. It enables practice supervisors, freed from organizational anxieties, to concentrate exclusively on developing the talents of the team. And conversely it enables those with skill in organization and administration to develop systems and procedures to enhance the smooth running of the office. Yet in operation, this co-management policy is extraordinarily difficult to manage. First, it offers limitless opportunities for the co-managers to be played off against each other. Second, if there are differences of approach, they will be artificially magnified in a situation which requires complete mutual understanding. Third, there is a real and inescapable tension between the administrative requirement to get work allocated and the desire to ensure high standards of practice. Where this tension is contained within one individual, it guarantees a rough balance. Where it is divided, it guarantees conflict. Like all structures, it can be operated given individuals with a shared commitment to seeing that it does work. But as a model it cannot be recommended.

The adviser role developed in fashion with the advent of large multi-purpose departments. It can best be understood as a response on the part of departments wishing to embrace wholeheartedly the generic concept, but recognizing at the same time the loss of expertise and skill which might result. The creation of adviser/consultant posts outside the line management structure was the uneasy compromise. Like the consultant role described above in the context of casework practice, the specialist adviser occupies an uncertain managerial position. Invested by the agency with a privileged position based on special skills and knowledge, the adviser yet has to reconcile his role with that of the line manager – and ultimately to cede authority to him. The end product of such a role is frequently confusion. Parsloe and Stevenson summarize: 'the general picture of the use of these specialists is a gloomy one. When used at all by social workers they are seen as a last resort in impossible situations and usually seen as failing to produce the necessary magic' (Parsloe and Stevenson 1978: 197). Social workers used advisers only in relation to resource availability, for example a place in a residential home, never in relation to behavioural patterns or pathology typical of a client group.

Before considering an example of how change can be effected through a team, it may be helpful to summarize the main arguments of the chapter so far. First, there are several different patterns of team organization. The choice made will depend upon the attitude of the team leader, the skills and experience of the team, the ethos of the department, and the pattern of work. A participative style is advocated in order to maximize the contribution of the team. Second, the team leader has opportunities to influence the development of the team through his use of allocation processes, team meetings, and projects. Whatever style is adopted, there is an inescapable teaching role. Third, it has been argued that (despite the work pressures) it is better for the supervisory and organizational elements of management to be handled by one individual rather than shared between team leaders, advisers, and consultants.

Bringing about change

It is always difficult to bring about change. An example of change in a team may serve to illustrate the conceptual framework of teamwork discussed earlier, as well as the skills required of the team leader in coping with the various interests groups affected. An area social services officer retired early. His retirement was part personal choice (having recently lost his wife, he wished to move away from the area to live near his daughter) and part managerial encouragement. Although a man of considerable charm, he had little awareness of management needs, was unable to encourage or inspire his staff, and tended to adopt a cheerful *laissez-faire* approach to every situation in the hope that the problems would go away. The newly appointed Area Officer thus came to an area demoralized and run down with a high proportion of long-serving but unqualified officers. Some desultory efforts had been made to improve the situation. A management consultant had been hired nine months earlier but his recommendations for change had been felt to be unrealistic and were ignored. His report had however helped to sharpen awareness of the problems.

The Area Officer thus came to a traditional team, but came at a time when there was a sense of change already in the air. The departmental senior management was clearly seeking a fresh approach. The area team itself, while unable to agree upon the implementation of the consultant's recommendations, had not challenged his diagnosis and looked with hope to the new area officer to provide miraculous solutions to long-standing problems. The workload of the area, dominated by referrals of elderly and handicapped clients, was not being dealt with speedily and a backlog had built up. With direct allocation from Area Officer to senior social workers, and from seniors to social workers, social work assistants, and occupational therapists, there were strong feelings about inbalances between staff workloads.

The newly appointed Area Officer felt it important to have a period of *orientation* for himself as he tested out the accuracy of the daily gripes which he received. But he decided to use the team itself as part of the orientation process. When statistics on workloads were produced, they were discussed in an area meeting. When the backlog of elderly referrals was examined, that examination took place in an area meeting. And when differing organizational patterns were considered, that too was done in the context of an area meeting. By this approach the team leader was able to achieve two objectives. First, he was able to dispel the fantasy about the miracle cure by exposing his own need to know more. Second, by sharing information, he created a sense of participation in the problems of the team by all the staff.

This latter process was not easy, for open discussion laid bare the latent tensions in the area. Some of the older staff muttered comparisons with the predecessor Area Officer. Social work assistants, responsible for over two hundred review cases, compared their burden with the dozen or so children in care handled by some of the social workers. Occupational therapists complained that as soon as a handicapped client crossed the office threshold they were certain to get the referral whatever the nature of the problem presented. This stage of *accommodation* as staff respond to a new pattern contains the element of 'jockeying' for position. It is often characterized by the emergence of *ad hoc* temporizing solutions as happened here. The backlog of elderly clients was shared evenly across the fieldwork staff – a suggestion made by a social work assistant, and enthusiastically endorsed by the team – amounting to only two clients each. And the Area Officer decided – despite the time commitment involved – to introduce an area allocation meeting on a time-limited basis specifically to tackle issues of which cases were appropriately handled by the different groups of fieldwork staff.

The next style of development thus saw open discussion and *negotiation* of the respective roles and responsibilities of staff. This greatly threatened the unqualified social workers. While previously secure in their status as social workers, and in the primacy which that role was accorded in the area, they now found their position undermined by the Area Officer's lack of readiness to accept their differential status. In many ways, this was the most difficult problem facing the Area Officer. He decided to tackle it in a number of ways. First, the area meeting decided to set up a project group to look at workload management and a long-serving unqualified officer was appointed as chairman. This formal recognition helped him to feel that his contribution to the area was still valued despite the changes. Second, an older officer with particular expertise in working with alcoholics, but whose skill had been taken for granted for many years, was encouraged to lead a discussion in an area meeting, and from that to write a short piece for the departmental newsletter. A third was given an explicit role as consultant in community resources. In summary, the Area Officer consciously set out to give them roles which were important to the evolving team, but which reflected the knowledge which they had acquired over the years.

In a relatively short time, some 3–4 months, the Area Officer had thus dealt with the backlog of work, found a way of involving the long-serving officers who constituted a potential resistance to any changes in team functioning, and had helped to promote a greater sense of corporate responsibility. But the changes did not affect only the fieldwork staff. The clerical staff had shared in the general demoralization of the office, and were influenced by the more optimistic attitudes pervading the team. From his previous experience, the Area Officer knew that the clerical staff held the key to office morale and were not merely reactive. He decided therefore actively to involve them in the changes under way. He insisted that clerical staff took a part in the project group looking at workload management, that the crucial role of clerical support in allocation meetings was fully recognized, and encouraged clerical staff to contribute in the area meeting. One meeting was devoted to the subject 'Reality and Fantasy – what a social worker can reasonably expect from clerical support'.

The *operational* stage of the changes introduced did not come about as a natural continuum from the initial process of orientation. The different attitude and use of clerical staff, the explicit roles for long-serving staff, and the use made of area meetings each in turn generated resistance – resistance which frequently went through stages of accommodation and negotiation before progress was made. The Area Officer felt however that the earlier stages were a necessary process before the team as a whole could contemplate any significant changes in organizational patterns, or area priorities. Having done so, the team could now collectively face these issues and reach its own decisions.

The example presented above is one which shows the value of a participative approach to management. It must be acknowledged that it begs a number of questions. Not all teams have the skills and resources among team members to create a genuine collaboration. Not all teams will respond in the way sought by the Area Officer, who then faces the ultimate dilemma of the participation-oriented manager – who takes the final decision when the Area Officer is out of step with the team? And not all teams have the basic harmony of approach from which collaborative working can flow.

Yet without a participative approach it is virtually impossible for the organizational structure to reflect the shared values and shared professional identity which characterizes social work. While there will be occasions – the imposition of a management policy of not filling vacancies, for example – when the Area Officer has to fulfil his responsibility as a manager despite team opposition, he will know the

Joint effort.

dangerous consequences of imposing unilateral policy decisions and will strive to ensure that all relevant staff are involved in prior discussion. The collaborative approach reflects social work values by according worth to each member of staff, by seeking to share both power and responsibility, and by breaking down the rigid boundaries of status and job definition.

The development of a greater degree of sharing in a team is not easily accomplished. The very pattern of work in agencies, based almost invariably on problems presented by individuals or families, encourages an individualized approach. Evans (1978) argues that the unitary perspective can help to combat this by promoting joint team work rather than individualized teamwork, a conceptualization which is akin to the community and traditional teams in Payne's classification. Drawing on research in probation office teams, he suggests that the maintenance of harmonious personal relationships is accorded a high priority with the result that conflicts and disagreements are rarely openly expressed. In individualized teamwork there are few joint decisions so harmony can readily be sustained, but the sharing of decision-making responsibility necessary for joint team work means that direct attention has to be paid to areas of disagreement.

Within the hierarchical structure of many social work agencies, how possible is it to reach a true sharing of decision-making? The emphasis on securing objectives has to cease being the exclusive prerogative of management. As the responsibility is a shared one, group support and group censure have to supplement the authority of the team leader as the means to achieve the collectively agreed goals. The organizational context in which collaborative working can best be developed is considered in the next chapter.

6

Organization and structure

The Seebohm Report (1968) was the decisive influence in producing the organizational structure of social work in England and Wales. Following in the wake of the Kilbrandon Report (1964) which had undertaken a similar task in Scotland, and which had in turn led to the 1968 Social Work (Scotland) Act, the committee chaired by Lord Seebohm explored a number of organizational solutions to the problems of offering social services which would reach out to the community. The solutions were geared to the problems of the existing provision in separate departments, which the report defined in terms of volume, range and quality, poor access, insufficient adaptability, and divided responsibilities. It is interesting, with the benefit of ten years' hindsight, to look at the options considered and discarded before the committee decided to recommend a social service department.

Seebohm's options

The alternative options to those finally recommended were:

(a) *Further research and experiment before a decision:* the classic evasion for politicians, but rightly rejected as irrelevant procrastination.
(b) *Existing structure with more formalized machinery for co-ordination:* an attractive solution, but rejected because of the problems of a co-ordinating committee without executive powers, and its lack of impact on fieldwork practice.
(c) *Two departments – one for services to children and families, one for the*

elderly and handicapped: this was rejected as perpetuating the symptom-centred approach to family problems, preventing treatment of family needs as a whole, and impairing continuity of care.

(d) *A social casework department acting on an agency basis for other departments:* this was rejected as artificially splitting social work from service provision and perpetuating divisions between departments.

(e) *Absorption into enlarged health departments:* this was rejected as impractical. The social care services, argued the report, needed concentrated attention without the distraction of other service demands.

(f) *Removal of social services from local government:* this was felt to be outside the committee's terms of reference, but in any event was rejected as failing to acknowledge the importance of citizen participation.

Of these options, the last three have remained as possible developments and have from time to time been advocated by different interest groups. But despite the heavy battery of criticism which has been directed against social work, there has been far less criticism of the basic organizational structure implemented after the Seebohm Report. It is worth considering, however, the attractions of removing social services provision from local government, for this proposition has been taken up by a number of social workers.

The reasons for its attraction can be simply summarized. First, the local government structure has bureaucratized social service provision; second, the vagaries of political control mean that resource allocation is subject to radical shifts according to the whims of the electorate; third, the hierarchical model of local government is inappropriate for social work practice; and fourth, as Peter Townsend argued to the BASW conference in 1981 when reviewing a decade of social services in local government, 'departments had been subordinated to central power and the scope and influence of SSD's had been carefully restricted and their resources controlled through corporate management.'

Yet the absence of alternative locations weakens the force of these arguments. The uneasy mix of central government and local government financial responsibility, administered by a lay committee, which characterizes the probation service is unlikely to command support, and is being questioned as an appropriate model for the changing character of probation (Haxby 1978). Regional structures were introduced to plan residential services for children, but the structure of Children's Regional Planning Committees has been ineffective, bedevilled by the rising costs of provision and local authority rivalries over pooling. The occasional flirtation of DHSS Ministers with a reorganization embracing both health and personal social services in one unified service offers only a more cumbrous bureaucratic structure, with less public accountability and the likelihood of medical domination. The most recent alternative is discussed in both the Nodder Report (1979) and *Care in the Community* (DHSS 1981b). This envisages a single authority responsible for the planning, provision, and management of services for a client group. The elderly, the mentally ill, and the mentally handicapped are the groups considered by the DHSS. While this presents a neat administrative model, the complexity of splitting off services to one client group to a different management structure is formidable. Furthermore any solution which weakened local authority control and direct public accountability would be bitterly resisted by local government interests.

Seebohm's proposals

The Seebohm Committee was constrained by its terms of reference from looking at structures outside local government. It chose instead to concentrate its prescription on the detailed operation of the social services department, and argued for a community-based social service administered from area offices serving a population of between 50–100,000. Together with the area team the report advocated the delegation of the maximum authority for decisions to the area offices. At area team level, the Seebohm prescription has been followed with remarkable fidelity, with the only exceptions being rural areas with a very scattered population and a handful of urban local authorities which have adopted an area office pattern but serving much smaller population groups. The striking differences between local authorities have occurred in senior management structures rather than in area teams.

The major variable determining structure is size – size of the area and size of the population served. The greater the geographical area served, the greater the degree of delegated authority which is likely to be given to the area or division. The other significant variable is based on the ideological stance of the agency towards residential work. Where this is seen as part of a continuum involving fieldwork and as a flexible resource, there will be a predisposition to link residential, day care, and fieldwork services at a relatively low level of the managerial hierarchy. But where these are seen as radically different resources, the tendency is likely to be to express this in managerial terms by a division of responsibility according to function.

Management structures

Before considering the two most common structures, based on geographical and functional divisions respectively, one should note the possibility of a managerial division on client group lines. While this was anathema in the early seventies as the newly created departments wholeheartedly embraced the generic concept, there is an increasing shift towards client groups as the basis for a cluster of management functions. Some area teams have been organized on client group lines, an echo of option (c) considered by the Seebohm Committee, and a handful of departments have carried this through into senior management structures with Assistant Directors taking overall responsibility for services to a client group. The divisions characteristically are elderly and handicapped, mental disorder, and children and families.

Far more usual however is a geographical organization. Here the respective Assistant Directors take responsibility for a particular geographical area and for all the services within it. Such a structure is geared more to the needs of a rural community. The broad responsibilities of the Assistant Director mean that this structure often correlates with a relatively small headquarters staff with decentralized decision-making. At the other end of the spectrum one finds a functional division of service responsibilities – fieldwork, residential, day care and domiciliary services, research and training. This functional model is the most frequently used organizational structure.

There is currently a wave of restructuring, but sadly this often owes more to considerations of economy than to rationality – which is the reason for the fierce resistance which restructuring proposals generate. What then are the rational considerations which should underlie decisions about organizational structures? The size of the area served has already been mentioned as a factor, with geographical divisions seeming somewhat artificial in a tightly knit urban area, but a logical way of coping with the problems of a scattered rural community. The weakness of a geographical structure lies in its inability to achieve consistency of procedures and practices throughout the department. With no overall co-ordination except at Director level, there is ample scope for very different policies to develop. While the initial reaction may be to welcome local initiative and to argue that local policies are developed to meet local needs, social services departments as a local government service have to recognize the need for territorial justice. The same people who argue for local autonomy would be at the forefront of protests if the same policy were applied in education, with grammar schools and secondary moderns in Conservative-held areas of a local authority and comprehensive schools in areas controlled by the Labour Party. Territorial justice dictates that similar criteria for the delivery of services must apply throughout the local authority. A functional structure in which one Assistant Director is responsible for all fieldwork provision is the surest way to achieve that objective.

The obvious weakness of a functional structure is the division between service areas, which in some ways it legitimizes. It amounts to an explicit managerial statement that the needs of fieldwork services, residential care, day care and domiciliary services are very different and demand different managerial approaches. It means that the cross-over point between the sectors of the department is again at Director level with the liability that only the Director has the power to resolve the inevitable conflicts of interest which will arise. Even at lower levels in the hierarchy, there may be limited communication between those with management responsibility for the various sectors of the department since each has a different allegiance.

Each of these management structures therefore has its weaknesses. Some authorities have devised structures which attempt to overcome the problems by integrating responsibility for field and residential services at Assistant Director level – as in the geographical model – but augmented by functional Assistant Directors at headquarters who have the responsibility for securing overall consistency in policy throughout the department. The potential conflict between the operational Assistant Director and the 'policy' Assistant Director will be evident, with its resolution owing more to force of personality than to the rightness of the argument. Another possible solution is to link geographical and client group responsibilities, with each Assistant Director responsible for a given geographical area and for services to a specific client group on a department-wide basis. The issue posed by this structure is how far the Assistant Director's client group responsibility is compatible with his colleagues' responsibility for staff in the area. If the Assistant Director for children insists that all child abuse referrals are seen on the day of referral, this has an immediate impact on priorities for other client groups and on the workload of the area teams, yet these are the managerial responsibilities of his colleagues.

This brief description of the structures most commonly used proffers no solutions. There is no ideal. All structures are imperfect, demanding a high degree of co-operation and co-ordination if they are to operate effectively. It is important, however, to dispel any illusion that there is a remedy to the ills of social services departments by tinkering with management structures.

Patchwork

It is particularly important to stress that no ideal exists when political enthusiasm presents patchwork as the answer to the organizational problems of social work agencies. It was observed in the previous chapter that the vogue for patchwork must evoke a strong sense of déja vu in those who recall the pre-Seebohm days, when it was the normative pattern of social work delivery. Why then has it become so fashionable to espouse the virtues of utilizing community resources? The rhetoric has changed little. The Seebohm Report visualized that area-based teams would provide statutory services with the key to unlock the treasures of citizen participation, but somehow that concept was never translated into action as departments – perhaps understandably – were preoccupied with their internal problems. The cold draught of cut-backs served to concentrate managerial minds wonderfully, and the current zeal for community-based solutions (while perfectly reputable in social work terms) has to be attributed to the recognition that the expansion of statutory provision is at an end for the foreseeable future.

The analysis endorsed by Patrick Jenkin, former Secretary of State for Social Services, has been most clearly stated by Hadley and McGrath. 'Most of these in need of care in the community – the frail elderly, the physically and mentally sick and handicapped, children at risk and others are supported not by the state but by families, friends and neighbours. . . . The aim of the social services departments should be to support these sectors, not to replace them' (Hadley and McGrath 1980: 10). From this basis, the role of social services is seen to be that of supporting voluntary care, of providing direct care for those who need it, and of recognizing the importance of breaking down barriers between the community and the professionals. Translating those concepts into practice requires a radical shift in professional attitudes.

Hadley and McGrath (1980) identify seven characteristics of a community-based method of organization. They are:

(a) *Locally-based teams, focusing on small areas or patches:* The pattern of area offices widely adopted in the wake of the Seebohm Report was for an area to serve a population between 50–100,000. Patch teams therefore imply the creation of sub-offices or outposted social workers to foster community links.

(b) *The capacity to obtain detailed information about the patch:* Obtaining better information about both community needs and community resources is seen as a primary objective of patch-based structures, with a strong emphasis placed on informal contacts.

(c) *Accessibility and acceptability to the patch population:* The basis of patchwork consists in workers becoming well known in the area, but goes beyond this to require the active involvement of local people in the delivery of services.

(d) *Close liaison with other local agencies and groups:* The emphasis placed on maximizing local resources demands close involvement with a wide range of voluntary organizations and groups.

(e) *Integration of all field and domiciliary services within patch teams:* Although not all patch teams achieve this integration owing to the separation of fieldwork and domiciliary services, Hadley and McGrath argue that high levels of information-sharing and co-operative working can best be achieved by formal integration of these services.

(f) *Participative management:* This is characteristic of the patch systems considered, with a high degree of staff involvement covering both fieldwork and administrative staff. Team meetings, 'away days' (evaluation days away from the office to look at the team and its development) and supportive relationships are the means whereby participative approaches are utilized.

(g) *Substantial autonomy exercised by patch and area teams:* While this is seen as desirable, the degree to which it was attained in the teams studied by Hadley and Mcgrath varied considerably.

Not all these characteristics will be present in every area which has opted for a community-based orientation, but they describe the necessary attitudes if such a shift is to prove effective. An important element is the recognition that social work in the sense of casework is not sought by the majority of social services clients, whose needs will better be met by domiciliary services or by community networks. This is most evident in the case of the elderly where Goldberg's (1978b) findings indicated the dubious utility of review visiting. She suggested that the social work role with the elderly would often be most far-reaching in its impact if social workers concentrated on creating and sustaining networks of support around the vulnerable elderly. As the elderly are the largest client group of departments, the implications of this approach for area services are considerable.

Writing of their experience in Nottinghamshire, Currie and Parrott (1981) provide a vivid account of the introduction of a patch system. Their theoretical perspective of a unitary approach underlies their description. By patch they mean something rather different to the use of the term by Hadley and McGrath. Their concept is of a group of workers responsible for a specific geographical area, not individual workers responsible for small communities. This differentiation is very important. At times the proponents of patch systems seem in danger of doing little more than substituting a generic community worker for the generic social worker. In Nottinghamshire, Currie and Parrott felt that 'by concentrating a team of social workers within a patch this could lead to the build up of knowledge of that area, of organisations within it and the pattern of social networks' (Currie and Parrott 1981).

The practical steps taken to translate the concept into reality warrant further discussion. They involved a conscious emphasis on information collection, looking at the available resources, local groups, social networks, and community leaders. Specific tasks were allocated to individual workers. From this information the team was able to identify the strengths of the community and appreciate the ways in which localized help was offered. The involvement of neighbours, volunteers, and clients in this process of giving help has been a significant factor in enabling the community to identify with the social services rather than seeing the department as an impersonal welfare bureaucracy.

Currie and Parrott describe their efforts to build up relationships within the community with voluntary agencies and groups. Informal contacts, exchanges, and lunchtime discussions were among the methods used. A liaison scheme was set up with local schools which enhanced the potential contribution of the team by receiving referrals of problems at an earlier stage, by helping in the development of community service projects, and by helping with courses on personal development and child care. Again, as with information collection, specific liaison functions were given to designated individuals with social workers taking responsibility for work with the DHSS, with the police, with schools and other significant organisations.

The patch model, however, is not something that one worker alone can implement. True, he can identify, develop, and utilize community resources and networks, but unless his approach is backed by management and complemented by colleagues it is unlikely to have any significant impact. The team approach advocated by Currie and Parrott is clearly that of the community team in the typology discussed in the preceding chapter. They define it as 'a group of social workers, social work assistants and a team leader sharing a collective responsibility for all social work activity in a prescribed geographical area'. By using the team as a whole, specializations within it could be encouraged and a truly generic social work service could be offered – but with the total spread of work covered by the whole team, and not by any one individual.

While the team has a collective accountability for work, it is argued by Currie and Parrott that there is also 'an emphatic pattern of individual accountability in all aspects of work directly to the team leader, and for the team leaders directly to the Area Director'. But the nature of the team approach dictates a more complex pattern of accountability than can be found in simple line management, for the team has a form of accountability to the local community and to community groups as well.

What all the structures do have in common is an assertion of the central position of the area team as the primary point of contact between the community and the department. The major argument within departments has not been about a challenge to that primacy, but about how staff can most effectively be organized. The Seebohm Report, having once indicated its support for unification, logically resisted the perpetuation of old specialisms in the new department and argued that 'a family or individual in need of social care should, as far as is possible, be served by a single social worker . . . the worker would of course be able to seek advice from colleagues but attempts at planning by committees of workers, none of them with a clear primary responsibility, should not be necessary' (Seebohm Report 1968: paras 516, 517). The interpretation of those words provoked much con- troversy, and still influences the pattern of development.

Specialization

Departments tended to go enthusiastically for the new generic approach, with caseloads being vigorously mixed as specialists were obliged to tackle wholly unfamiliar tasks. Confusion was rampant. But by the end of the decade, the range of tasks to be performed no longer held the terrors that it had for unprepared child care officers, psychiatric social workers, and welfare officers. And new patterns of specialization had indeed begun to emerge. Parsloe and Stevenson (1978) found that patterns of specialization were a preoccupation of the social work teams which they studied in their research. Two particular influences on specialization were identified. First, the size of an area or team was important in determining the use of specialists. Intake teams were more frequently found in larger areas with a heavy burden of referrals. Formal specialization by client group, or indeed by method, was felt to be far more difficult to operate in small teams. Second, the type of staff employed influenced the development of specialist skills. If a large number of social work assistants were employed, work with the elderly was rarely undertaken by the social workers themselves, thus effectively precluding the development of a specialism in that area. If occupational therapists were employed, most work with the handicapped was allocated to them, again militating against the development of specialist social work skills.

INTAKE AS A SPECIALIZATION

The most significant new specialization to emerge is that of intake work. This was initially developed as a vehicle to cope with the flow of referrals. Whereas a high proportion of work by child care officers and mental welfare officers had been long-term in its nature, the workload of social services departments has a very different pattern. Goldberg and colleagues found a quarter of referrals disposed of on the first day, and nearly 50 per cent within a week (Goldberg and Warburton 1979). The community orientation of departments encouraged referrals. The research of Reid and Shyne (1969) had considerable influence throughout social work in emphasizing the potential benefits of focused and time-limited intervention. Thus considerations of practice and of expediency came together to stimulate the development of intake work as a specialism, emphasizing assessment skills and focused work. The volume of work dealt with enabled intake workers swiftly to build up experience, to develop good links with referring agencies, and to identify those clients where long-term intervention would be needed. In some areas, intake teams utilized crisis theory to promote change in a client and operated from a different theoretical perspective from their colleagues in long-term teams.

Despite this organizational specialization, it is rare to find intake workers describing themselves as specialist workers. Buckle (1981), however, has argued that intake work is a valid specialism, and should be developed as such within the organizational context of social services departments. Several probation areas have changed their method of working to develop specialist roles in court-work and report-writing. Nevertheless the designation of specialist worker has tended to remain associated primarily with those specializing in work with a particular client group. 'Almost without exception, when asked about informal specialization at team level, social workers responded by talking about the bias in their caseloads towards particular client groups' (Parsloe and Stevenson 1978: 171). Most social workers do have some bias within their caseloads whatever the organizational pattern of the area. The bias may reflect personal preferences for work with particular groups, the propensity of the locality in which they are working to produce particular clusters of problems (e.g. depression and financial hardship in a community where the principal source of employment shuts down), or the previous experience of the worker.

CHILDREN AND FAMILIES AS A SPECIALIZATION

The most widely found specialist role is work with children and families. This reflects the increasingly dominant position of the former child care specialism within social services departments. Two influences here have been the importance accorded to statutory work when priorities have been set, and the impact of guidance following inquiries into child care tragedies. Unlike other areas of social work practice, the legislature has provided a detailed framework for the execution of child care supervision right down to prescribing the frequency of visits to children in care. As resources have become more limited, adherence to those requirements has been regarded as a higher priority than regular contact with other arguably more needy clients where no statutory prescription exists. The media coverage of the Colwell case and its successors has reinforced the determination of social services managements to be 'fire proof' in this area of work.

As a consequence of this preoccupation with children, which is also shared by social work students whose declared preferences for specialization put work with children as a top choice, the specialisms which have emerged often relate to sub-groups of child care practice – fostering and adoption, intermediate treatment, children in care, group-work with lone parents, and pre-school work. In some areas these specialist roles have been so developed that all work coming from that category is hived off from the general practice of the area team. While this can lead to the development of expertise and good standards of work, it can also pose problems for management. First, it is necessary to work at processes of co-ordination and ensure that ready communication exists between the specialists and the generalists. Second, it can impair morale among the area team workers if popular, rewarding and prestigious areas of practice are progressively removed.

By contrast with the hiving off of popular areas of work, the converse process took place in relation to the blind and deaf. For these clients, the zeal with which genericism was embraced led to the dilution of the highly specialized service which they had formerly enjoyed. Yet social workers did not fill the gap left by the former technical officers, and Parsloe and Stevenson found 'little attempt to distinguish between tasks which might be performed by someone possessing specific teaching skills which are not necessarily part of social work and that part of the problem of visual handicap which necessitates social work activity' (Parsloe and Stevenson 1978: 184).

SPECIALIZATION BY TASK AND SKILL

One of the most intriguing aspects of the development of social services departments has been the evolving role of occupational therapists. The passage of the Chronically Sick and Disabled Persons Act (1970) at the beginning of the decade and the International Year of the Disabled at the end of the decade provide the context for examining how far departments have progressed in meeting the needs of the handicapped. The truth is that despite financial constraints, despite the relative lack of priority from social workers, and despite the criticisms of the highly vocal disability lobby, an immense amount has been achieved. The numbers of aids supplied, adaptations undertaken, domiciliary services available, care attendant schemes initiated, and day centre places created have increased very substantially. What has not happened, however, is any significant clarification of the social work role with the handicapped, notwithstanding CCETSW's explicitly titled *People with Handicaps Need Better Trained Workers* (CCETSW 1974).

Occupational therapists like social workers resist being labelled as the people who help with aids, but few departments are yet geared to utilize their professional skills in helping disabled persons with problems of rehabilitation. Here there is potential overlap with the role of the social worker in dealing with the emotional problems associated with disability, an overlap which can be used positively in a team approach by recognizing that each worker can offer different skills to meet different needs, or it can be used as justification for a 'one client, one worker' approach which ends up by diluting the total service offered.

This is not to deny the benefit of specialization. While the total workload of a department is broadly based, it is wholly unrealistic to expect social workers to display equal competence in all areas of practice. It is important, however, to eliminate multiple visiting as far as this is consistent with skilled and knowledgeable service provision. It is important to recognize the common base of practice in skills of assessment and of relationship, and to be ready to transfer knowledge from one complex of social problems to another group where there are factors in common. That means that the basis of practice in area *teams* should be generic while affording opportunities for specialization within the team. How that specialization is organized most effectively then becomes the critical issue.

Sainsbury argues persuasively that:

'the development of specialization needs to be *preceded* by the development of generic teams and team caseloads whereby, although one worker would continue to orchestrate the inputs of work for each case, and would provide continuity of experience for clients, all workers would be encouraged to develop personal areas of expertise relative to specific tasks and skills within the total range of work responsibilities allotted to the team.'   (Sainsbury 1980)

Such an approach offers the possibility of achieving a synthesis of what is best in the collaborative teamwork of social work and what is best in the development of skill and expertise. It can be argued therefore that the basic concept of the Seebohm Report for a generalist approach has been vindicated. In some areas it has fallen into disrepute, but usually this is because of misguided enthusiasm in the implementation of generic social work, as a consequence of which the 'generic social worker' has become the scapegoat for all the ills of social services departments.

To develop specialization on the basis of tasks and skills raises the elusive issue of what the skills peculiar to social work are. The BASW document on *The Social Work Task* (BASW 1977), the Local Authority Associations Study Group, and most recently the Barclay Inquiry have all attempted to look at the boundary areas between social work and other disciplines. In order of frequency of use as reported by clients, Sainsbury found the most frequently used inputs to be encouragement/support, negotiation/advocacy, financial help, insight techniques, advice, exercise of authority, and rehearsal of events (e.g. job interviews, social security appeals). His research findings also illustrated the pervasive influence of the agency itself in determining the nature of the response (Sainsbury 1980).

Three illustrations of this will suffice. Local authority social workers were markedly unsuccessful in handling clients' financial problems whereas Family Service Unit workers achieved significant improvements, reflecting the long-standing concern of that organization with material deprivation. Probation Officers were both more sensitive to the existence of marital problems and more effective in offering help, reflecting probation's traditional involvement with matrimonial work. By contrast, where the work involved mother–child relationships, the focus on child care in local authority services led to a more effective intervention by these workers than by others.

The research findings by Sainsbury indicate that an effective team needs to be aware of the way in which the underlying ethos and values of the agency and its context influence perception and practice. In particular, more needs to be done to develop skills in welfare benefits advice, collaborative working with other agencies, employment assistance, the development of informal support networks, and in social skills training if the needs of clients are to be matched by skills in workers. The team approach described by Currie and Parrott comes closest to meeting this ideal, but poses challenges to social work management. First, the sharing inherent in the approach builds a formidable group which may threaten centralized and controlling management structures. Second, the team leader, the Area Officer and the Director have to accept a loss of power as the team becomes the focus for service initiatives. Third, no single team leader can hope to encompass the range of skills needed in the team. He may therefore need to supplement his own supervisory skills by using group supervision, or peer supervision where two colleagues mutually accept supervisory responsibility for the other – a pattern well fitted to those in highly specialized roles.

Outposting

If the debate about the wisdom of the Seebohm Report's recommendations in relation to generic work in area teams continues to rage, that on another of its recommendations in its chapter on specialization has been far more muted. The recommendation that social workers should be attached on a fairly long-term basis to institutions such as schools, health centres, courts, and hospitals while continuing to be based on the social services department has received little attention. If implemented on a substantial basis it could undermine the area team as the focal point of social work intervention, and the primacy of the area team has gone virtually unchallenged hitherto. This outposting role undeniably presents problems both to social work managements and to the individual worker. While the worker lacks the support and stimulus of close association with professional colleagues, management lacks any detailed knowledge of the worker's performance and has to establish a delicate working contact with the management of the other setting – be they head teachers, GPs in a health centre, or the management committees of a community project.

Yet outposting does offer great potential to influence other settings. GPs, not traditionally great enthusiasts for social work, nevertheless value the contribution which an attached worker can make in a group practice. While that may owe something to the view of social work's role as essentially supportive to health care professionals, a skilled social worker can establish an independent niche while promoting the values of social work throughout the practice setting, which needs that influence to redress the inbalance inherent in the doctor–patient relationship. Similar conflicts exist in the school setting. The low status and poor level of qualification of education social workers, formerly known as education welfare officers, has militated against their acceptance as an independent discipline with something of value to contribute. Their separation from social services departments has denied them a potential power base. Instead pastoral care has developed as a teaching role. The merits of the latter development are still the source of controversy. The consequence, however, is that even where social workers perceive the structure and organization of school life to be fundamentally damaging to the development of some of its pupils, there is no ready channel for them to communicate that perception.

Bridging fieldwork and residential care

While the limited development of outposting has not eroded the supremacy of area teams as the focus for the delivery of services, there are signs that a more flexible approach to services is emerging in some departments. Allen, speaking to the conference of the Residential Care Association in 1977, said:

> 'the way we divide our services into separate management boxes does, in my view, put unnecessary obstacles in the way of a proper integration of all our resources. Generally speaking, each residential

establishment remains a separate outpost, serviced by and managed by people at some central office usually located in a different place from the servicing and managing of fieldwork, and of domiciliary and day care services.'

(Allen 1977)

Even in divisional structures considered earlier, there is usually only limited contact between fieldwork and residential staff.

The reasons for the gap are clear. The impact of Goffman's (1968) work on social work practice with its stress on the negative and damaging impact of institutions, the hangover from the Poor Law concept of the workhouse, an unrealistic view of the healing properties of community care, and latterly, awareness of the high financial cost of residential provision have combined to promote a view of residential care as a last resort. Fieldwork has offered higher levels of trained staff, better salaries, and immeasurably better career prospects. Yet a rigid division between the two settings is irrational, and glaringly so in relation to children in care where the goal should be continuity of relationship. In practice too often children in residential care have been subject to bewildering changes of worker, compounding their confusion and unhappiness.

It is worth looking at one local authority to see the way in which the evolution of services is subverting the dominant role of the area team as the locus for fieldwork services. In the last five years, children's homes, hostels for the mentally ill, hostels for the mentally handicapped, and an Adult Training Centre have all been used as the base for fieldwork provision. The concepts underlying this approach and the practical problems experienced are important, for they illustrate the issues to be confronted if residential and day care establishments are to be more widely used as resource centres for the clients whom they serve.

The first extension of the residential care role from that of providing a secure caring physical environment came with the decision to change the use of an observation and assessment centre to a long-stay children's home for older children in care. (One characteristic of bureaucracies is that it is far easier to innovate and break free from the mould of long-established practices when setting up a new establishment, but exceptionally difficult to do so when a change of policy is being applied to an existing establishment where precedents can be cited as resistance to change.) The basis of the structure proposed was that those in the residential setting should have full responsibility for all aspects of the care of the child. Instead of having uneasy and intermittent visits from social workers who were uncertain of their role with children in long-term care, the residential workers as a team operated autonomously with no fieldworker having any responsibility for the children.

One important element in this concept is the adoption of the *team*, rather than any individual residential worker, as the responsible body for each child in the establishment. This places a premium on ready communication between all staff, but is a logical extension of the specialization by skill and task discussed earlier. The twenty-four hours a day, seven days a week demands of residential care make the individual worker–child relationship a difficult model to operate, but the approach adopted does mean that the children can take what they need from the adult workers in the home. The responsibility for the child remains with the residential team after the child leaves the establishment, so that in addition to full responsibility for children placed in the home the staff discharge a fieldwork role in relation to ex-residents. At any time, therefore, the team will be caring for many more children in community placements of one kind or another than are actually resident in the home.

Applying this approach in children's homes brings problems in its wake. As described it is apposite only to those in long-term care where there is no realistic prospect of rehabilitation with natural parents, but it is possible to apply in other long-stay settings. The difficulties arise with more highly qualified fieldworkers reluctant to cede responsibility to often unqualified residential workers, and reluctant also to accept a concept of team responsibility where this is foreign to their usual way of working. A danger too is that the formal transfer of responsibility, while giving status to residential workers, can serve to accentuate the divide between residential and fieldworkers by removing any necessity to collaborate and communicate.

But it is not only from children's homes that fieldwork services are being offered. In mental handicap and mental illness hostels, staff roles have also undergone a change. As a result of an agreement with the housing department, a number of ordinary council tenancies have been made available each year for letting to clients coming from the hostels for the mentally handicapped and recovering mentally ill respectively. Often even when residents are ready to move on from the security of the hostel environment, they are ambivalent about the challenge of living unaided in the community. Sometimes dependent relationships have been established with hostel staff. The process of reintegration into normal patterns of community living can therefore best be helped by the hostel staff, who are familiar trusted faces. Residential social workers continue to offer support and help to growing numbers of former residents. Less difficulty has been experienced with fieldworkers over the relinquishment of this area of responsibility. The management problem is that with a substantial throughput of residents each year, the numbers cared for in the community quickly build up and need additional staffing provision if the group home programme is to be adequately supported.

A slightly different pattern prevails at the Adult Training Centre (ATC), where a worker is outposted to work with trainees and their families. The rationale here is simple. Families have of necessity a relationship with staff at the ATC as does the trainee. Those at the ATC spend many hours a week with the trainee and thus know the potential and the problems of each individual almost as well as the family. If the fieldwork with families were to operate from an area team a third axis would be interposed, and one less well placed to effect necessary change than staff based directly at the ATC.

The final illustration of how one local authority – little by little, and without any conscious intent – has restricted the fieldwork role of area teams comes again from the mental handicap field. Here a children's home was converted into a unit aiming to provide short-term residential care and a range of practical help to the families of mentally handicapped children, including 'baby sitting' services, holiday play schemes, day care, after-school care, and holidays. The flexible use of the unit extends to staff roles. There is a strong parents' group which is actively involved in the running of the unit, and a pool of volunteers who provide assistance. The staff may be sole workers having total responsibility for the child and family and their needs, or may be key workers whilst the continuing fieldwork responsibility remains with the area team, or in some instances the staff may be a resource providing a valuable service but with the responsibility resting with the area-based fieldworker. While such lack of definition might be anticipated as a source of potential difficulty, in practice it has worked exceptionally well and has served to diffuse some of the tensions experienced elsewhere where area team roles have been whittled down.

But while the examples have been drawn from one authority, they could be repeated many times over with the emerging role of residential establishments as 'resource centres', as bases from which an array of services including residential, day care, and fieldwork services can be offered. While no example of a geriatric resource centre has been cited, it is not difficult to imagine a more flexible establishment offering residential, short-stay, and day care as well as being a base for occupational therapy and social work services to the elderly. Developments of this kind not only modify traditional thinking about residential care. They also call into question any organizational structures which are based on clear-cut divisions between field and residential work.

This new flexibility is not an exclusive characteristic of local authority social services. In voluntary organizations and in the probation service, similar innovations are to be found. In particular, long-established voluntary child care organizations have courageously switched the focus of their activities from traditional patterns of residential provision to community-based approaches. Dr Barnardo's, the Church of England Children's Society, and the National Children's Homes have all embarked on intermediate treatment initiatives. The National Society for the Prevention of Cruelty to Children has established special units throughout the country, which have swiftly won a reputation as centres of excellence in dealing with child abuse.

The Barnardo's Chorley project was a seminal influence on the mental handicap establishment discussed above. With the basic aim of allowing mentally handicapped children and their families to live as normal a life as possible, Barnardo's established a group of social workers and agreed with the local authority that within the project area it would take over the visiting for all families with a severely handicapped child. A toy library, home sitting services, play schemes, holidays, and short-term care all followed – and as in the scheme previously described, the services are heavily dependent on volunteer input. As Shearer's account of the project concludes, 'the outlines of support services to parents have been drawn. All that is needed now is for more people willing to get on and provide them' (Shearer 1978). The reluctance of local authorities to meet that challenge may, it is suggested, be due to more than just the exigencies of financial restraint. It may be tied up with the very organizational structure which still dominates social services departments.

The probation service has, like voluntary organizations, shown a willingness to re-examine its whole *raison d'être* in the last decade. More so than other social work agencies, it has accepted the grim lessons of research – notably the IMPACT project in England and Wales (Folkard 1975 and 1976) and Martinson's (1974) literature survey – that probation supervision has no significant capacity to bring about change in the offenders under supervision. Bottoms and McWilliams have suggested that the probation service therefore needs to abandon its treatment orientation, and to concentrate on maintenance, support, and prevention of deterioration (Bottoms and McWilliams 1979). This policy of limited objectives has substantial implications for the present organizational structure of the service, which is still largely based on groups of officers working with an individual caseload of offenders.

The process of diversification from this structure has been continuing throughout the 1970s, as first the probation service moved into the prison system taking on responsibility for the welfare service previously administered on a voluntary basis, and subsequently took on responsibility for hostel provision, day training centres, bail hostels, and community service. Experiments with short-term treatment and social skills training have further moved the service away from its former emphasis on casework. Part of the switch is undoubtedly attributable to the desire of leaders of the service to see it recognized as the group responsible for all non-custodial approaches to delinquency. But the result of the switch is to force the service to adopt more flexible administrative structures.

Haxby (1978) has argued that the existing structure, still formally dependent on Probation and After-Care Committees drawn virtually exclusively from local magistrates, no longer reflects the new extended role of the service. He advocates the establishment of a Community Correction Board, which would be representative not only of the magistracy but of other interests. This might include local authority representation, representation from academic institutions, from other professional disciplines, from the local health authority, and from voluntary organizations. The provision of direct services to clients through area offices and services to courts would remain as a primary function of the service, but in addition the Board would be responsible for residential and day facilities, community-based projects, and developmental work.

Managerial response to change

This chapter has developed the argument that social work's organizational structure in Britain is changing. It is changing in response to
new approaches to social work practice which place less emphasis
than formerly on the individual worker–client relationship, and
changing too as a reaction against the rigidities of the bureaucratic
structures which have characterized social services departments.
How best to organize to facilitate good practice remains an open
question, but certain indicators do exist.

The change is underpinned by the concept of shared responsibility:
sharing within teams and sharing with voluntary helpers. But such a
change has major implications for the traditional view of accountability within local government as it cannot readily be reconciled with a
hierarchical management structure. By developing informal community resources, agencies risk a loss of control, a loss which is
threatening to both elected members and senior management. One
possible solution advanced by Sainsbury could be:

> 'a modified version of the probation case committee, where area
> teams of workers, in addition to their location and accountability
> within line management, are required to meet regularly with
> members of their appointing committee as representatives of wider
> community policies, and where powers of cooption are sometimes
> used to increase the representation of local neighbourhood in-
> terests.'
> (Sainsbury 1981)

In addition to the managerial problems posed by greater community involvement there are structural problems. Notwithstanding the
examples of successful patch teams (Hadley and McGrath 1980,
Currie and Parrott 1981), there is much evidence from the DHSS-
sponsored study of area teams (Parsloe and Stevenson 1978) that
social workers find it difficult to give equal emphasis to work with
individuals and families in need, and to work aimed at promoting the
welfare of the community. It may prove necessary to have workers
operating in specialist roles if the team as a whole is to give equal
emphasis to both strands of work.

What are the implications of these changes for middle managers,
area officers, and team leaders? First, while the supervisory aspect of
work will remain important, it is likely to be diversified with more use

made of group supervision, peer supervision, and live supervision. Second, the middle manager's role will increasingly be to help social workers to relate their work with individuals to the needs of the wider community by alerting workers to local resources, and by encouraging them to contribute to policy debates. Third, the middle manager has to draw together the wide range of interests and experiences in order to make the most use of the potential of the team. And above all, the middle manager has to remain responsive to innovative thinking and the development of new methods, especially on how best to involve local citizens in the structure of provision to create truly community-based services.

7

Planning

Hitherto the concentration of this book has been on the aspects of management directly related to practice. The manager as supervisor of an individual, the manager as leader of a team, and the manager as arbiter of organizational structures have been the focus of examination. But one of the lessons which has been learned by social services managers is that the management role takes in far more than professional practice, and the manager has also to develop skills in strategic planning, financial control, and in programming to cope with the more complex networks with which social work agencies are now involved.

Before the specific requirements of effective planning in social service agencies are considered, it is important to clarify the background to the planning process as a whole in the context of local government. In government agencies of all kinds, regardless of function, the annual budgetary process is the crucial influence on policy implementation. Despite the adoption of an array of techniques from PPBS (Planning-Programming-Budgeting Systems) to zero base budgeting, with many variants in between, the supremacy of the annual budget remains. This has been compounded by the bewildering shifts in public expenditure policies which have characterized central government's attitude to local government in recent years. Local authorities have been made the 'whipping boy' for spiralling public expenditure notwithstanding their excellent overall record in complying with expenditure targets set by central government.

Financing of local government

Local government is largely financed by the Exchequer. This apparent paradox is the result of the rate support grant whereby central government meets nearly three-fifths of approved expenditure. The recent switch to a block grant system is designed to remove the 'blank cheque' element of central support for all local authority spending, and to substitute in its stead a system which sets a target for grant-related expenditure on a service by service basis, and calculates grants on that basis. There are various mechanisms to modify the rough edges, but essentially the block grant system is a crude reversion to the doctrine that the man in Whitehall knows best, for grant-related expenditure is calculated for each local authority on the basis of outdated and unreliable statistics which are not subject to challenge by individual authorities.

The effect of the block grant system is to make the rates the only means whereby a local authority can finance local programmes in excess of its 'target' expenditure. Where it elects to do so, a substantial rate increase is inevitable as no supplementary source of finance is available. The political sensitivity of increasing the rates is likely further to emphasize the budgetary process as authorities seek to adjust expenditure to produce a level of rates which will be politically acceptable.

Despite the enthusiasm for corporate management which was evident in the early 1970s as local authorities following the Bains Report (1972) created powerful central departments, most local authorities have continued to prepare budgets entirely on a departmental basis with only a limited policy input from outside the particular department. The process starts early in the financial year with a decision at member level about the overall resources likely to be available for the following year. This decision will be informed by central government projections for local authority expenditure, by political considerations about the desirability of increasing or decreasing services, and by equal (and opposite) political considerations about acceptable rating levels. After this initial target is set, the individual departments work out the implications for their services.

It is generally accepted that the annual financial cycle is inappropriate to consistent policy-making and implementation both at central and local government level. But the White Papers on public expenditure in which the government sets out its projections and targets for individual programme areas have shifted so much from year to year, and latterly in mid-year too, that they represent a very flimsy base for medium-term financial and service planning. The jerky progress described as stop-go has been replaced by successive reductions in the overall planned level of public spending. The traditional incremental style of local authority budgeting in which Chief Officers entered claims for service developments, which were then assessed for relative priority, has been replaced by 'disincrementalism' in which the grisly consequences of service reductions are weighed against each other for relative priority. The revolution in attitude which this has wrought on long-serving local government officers is profound. For them, there are no verities left.

The budget process

The process of drawing up the budget starts with an examination of the cost of maintaining existing services. This needs to reflect the full-year cost of new schemes started during the current year, to take account of salary drift through job evaluation, and to reflect any differential factors like lower (or higher) levels of staff turnover. But in addition to the maintenance of existing service levels, local authorities usually have commitments of various kinds which have to be considered. First, there are many set standards to be maintained. Just as education authorities maintain a pupil–teacher ratio, some authorities like to keep services in line, for example, with the increasing numbers of elderly. There may therefore be a prior commitment to increase services to reflect demographic change. Second, there may be commitments arising from the Urban Aid programme or a similar central government initiative which has financial implications for local government. Third, there may be a capital project – a home, day centre, or hostel – planned three years previously but due to open in the year under review, for which budgetary provision has to be made. And fourth, the revenue consequences of joint financing have to be met. Joint financing is discussed below, but the essential principle is that the local authority assumes full financial responsibility for projects over a five- or seven-year period. In each year therefore additional revenue provision has to be made for joint financing.

Managers then have to decide how this additional expenditure is to be contained within the financial target. When the initial target contains an allowance for growth, this is relatively easy. When the target is of standstill, or reductions in expenditure, the initial estimates need to contain examples of how the savings can be made either by reduction of services or by increases in charges. With the state of uncertainty which now governs local government finance, departments are usually required to go a step further than drawing up one set of estimates. They are also required to state how they would use additional resources if the final target were more generous, or, more frequently in the current climate, to state how they would make cuts of 2, 4, 6, even sometimes 10 per cent if required.

CHOOSING PRIORITIES

The purpose of these illustrative examples of cuts is, of course to enable councillors to form a judgement on the relative priority of services within the departmental budget, but also to enable the Policy Committee (or its equivalent) to make judgements between the priority to be accorded to different service areas. The task of weighing a deterioration in the pupil–teacher ratio against cutting the home help service would test the judgement of Solomon – and in truth the judgements that are made are rarely informed by a high level of rational analysis weighing the cost effectiveness of different policies. For it is in the arena of political conflict, with Chief Officers and Chairmen anxious to protect their own interests, that crude horse-trading sometimes takes place.

A frequently used tactic of senior managers – albeit one now often recognized by experienced councillors – is to offer up savings in areas which the Committee will find unacceptable. Closure of luncheon clubs for the elderly or reducing the home care service or a cut with similar emotive overtones may be suggested in the knowledge that the Committee will either reject it, or that a strong public lobby will develop as a result of which the proposal will be abandoned. Members can be influenced by public opinion, but the influence tends to relate to specific proposals rather than the overall balance of spending between service areas. How then are these relative priorities determined?

Until recent years, the answer was often that they were not. Rather than embark on the invidious task of singling out one service area, many local authorities preferred to adopt a system of across the board cuts with similar percentage reductions applied to all services. It gave a form of rough justice, but the roughness has become more evident as local authorities have grown more conscious of the importance of demographic factors in dictating demand for education and social services. Thus education services have been catering for fewer and fewer pupils in the last five years while social services have been caring for more and more elderly, and especially very elderly.

The process by which priorities are determined reflects a number of disparate influences. Key officers in the authority – the Chief Executive and the Treasurer – are involved in discussions with the leader of the council both about the overall rate level and its distribution between services. The rate support grant negotiations, which are usually concluded in late November, are a major influence on the overall rate level. The strength of Chief Officers, the political weight carried by services, the pressure from back-bench councillors and Committee Chairmen are among the factors which will affect the distribution between service areas. What is here described is a coarse process but is what happens albeit in slightly different ways in the great majority of local authorities. There are however a handful of authorities which would lay claim to a rational allocation of available resources using tools of corporate analysis.

In the heady days of local government reorganization corporate management was a fashionable concept. It meant more than a small team of Chief Officers taking the major strategic decisions. It meant too a strong Chief Executive's office, freed from departmental responsibilities and able to undertake policy analysis. While there is no clear pattern for the organization of policy analysis, it often spreads across more than one department and is the product of work undertaken by inter-departmental corporate groups. The effectiveness of the approach is wholly dependent on the numbers and calibre of the staff given this role, but where a strong corporate planning unit is in existence it can have an enormous influence on both policy development and resource allocation. While most authorities continue to pay lip-service to a corporate approach, the cut-backs of staff have fallen disproportionately on units of this kind which have no executive responsibilities. Overall in local government, the effect of stringency has been to restore the previously waning influence of departmentalism and incrementalism.

Budgetary control

Hitherto the formation of the budget only has been examined, but in most authorities only a handful of senior managers are directly involved in this process. But when the budget has been agreed, it becomes the responsibility of service managers in the middle ranks to ensure that budgetary control is exercised. As has been argued, the changes in service budgets are changes at the margin. Most vote heads – the subdivisions of the budget which are rarely reported to Committee in detail – increase by the rate of inflation year on year. Residential care of the elderly might have up to fifty vote heads covering everything from staff salaries to maintenance of grounds, from supplies of food to staff travel, from periodicals and magazines to furniture and equipment. Each vote head has to be monitored, sometimes by the service manager, sometimes by central administrative staff, to ensure that spending is broadly on target. In local government, underspending is as great a sin as overspending. Not only does it weaken the case for resources in ensuing years, but any underspending goes to Council balances and not to the benefit of the particular service area.

How can spending be checked, and what can be done if it is wildly off target? There are two systems of regulating expenditure, which may be alternatives or may be complementary. First, simplest and most widely used, is a manual record of expenditure. This needs to include a record not merely of expenditure incurred but also of expenditure committed. Furniture, for instance, may be ordered and the expenditure thus effectively committed several months before payment actually has to be made. The officer responsible for monitoring the vote head should thus be able to know something of the likely pattern of future spending as well as the current position. The second system for monitoring expenditure is computer-based. All expenditure is processed through the main-frame computer, which produces at weekly or monthly intervals as required print-outs showing expenditure. It is not always as easy to interrogate a computer as an individual so that in many areas one finds two parallel record-keeping systems in operation.

If expenditure is running ahead of target, it can be controlled by cutting back on the level of provision or it can be accommodated within the overall departmental budget by transferring resources from an area which is underspending. This latter process is known as 'virement', but is subject to a number of constraints. First, the total sum which can be 'vired' is limited, at least without formal Committee approval. Second, virement is usually allowed only in a similar area of service. Savings on food in homes for the elderly could not be allocated to intermediate treatment, for instance, whereas savings on placements in community homes could be. Third, virement to salaries is usually not permitted, especially with the current sensitivity about manpower numbers.

Considerable emphasis has been placed on the budgetary process because of its dominant influence on service planning. It has been suggested that the worsening economic climate, reductions in local government spending, and the perceptible withdrawal from a corporate approach have contributed to the re-emergence of incremental planning. Social services have particular reason to be chary of planning with long time horizons, for the ten-year plans adopted in the early 1970s are now gathering dust in council archives throughout the land.

Ten-year plans and LAPS

Ten-year plans were not a new phenomenon for local authorities. In 1962 they had been required to produce ten-year plans for the development of health and welfare services, and in 1972 Sir Keith Joseph, then Secretary of State for Social Services, called upon local authorities to produce ten-year plans for social services. In these, authorities were asked to forecast capital and revenue expenditure over the ten years, to detail the premises and places they planned to provide and to project numbers of staff in post. The DHSS advised authorities to plan on the basis of a 10 per cent growth rate throughout the plan period, and with such cheery assumptions some magnificent projections for developing the fabric of social welfare were fed back to the department.

The unreality of the exercise was swiftly to become apparent. In December 1973, the first round of public expenditure cuts were undertaken, and in subsequent years the scale of cuts was to grow. It is important to accept that in most instances the cuts have been cuts in planned growth rather than cuts in the current budget. In personal social services, the initial reductions fell heavily on capital spending –

on new and replacement homes, hostels and day centres, leaving intact existing levels of staffing. But capital spending was at the very heart of local authorities' ten-year plans, which were filled with ambitious new projects to expand provisions. In three years capital expenditure was reduced to a third of its original level – and the plans assumed historical interest only.

But the advent of cuts in public spending was not the only reason for the failure of the ten-year plans. Local authorities themselves were sceptical of the value of the exercise even before the chill winds of restraint began to bite. They lacked the staffing capacity and expertise in social services departments to engage in sophisticated planning of this kind. The local authority associations and the Association of Directors of Social Services warned against a repetition of the exercise in 1974, a year when local government reorganization was in any event placing new burdens on staff in many authorities. Outside social services departments there was little enthusiasm for this exercise which appeared to go against the corporate approach to local government management which was being preached elsewhere.

It was 1977 before the DHSS again embarked on the task of seeking returns from local authorities setting out their plans for the development of social services. The Local Authority Planning Statement (known universally as LAPS) had its counterpart in housing, namely the Housing Investment Programme Submission (known as HIPS), leading to much ribald comment among the staff charged with completing the returns. The timescale of LAPS was more modest than formerly with returns required for three years. The task of local authorities was eased too by the issue of a DHSS consultative document, *Priorities for Health and Personal Social Services in England* (DHSS 1976), which laid down growth rates for individual service areas compatible with the more restricted level of spending likely to be available.

This return was only marginally more successful than its predecessor. It survived for two years only. The first year's return was used as the basis for feedback to local authorities, and enabled authorities to compare their performance with other authorities with broadly similar characteristics using cluster analysis techniques. In the second year authorities were asked to amplify their returns with a strategy statement. There was however a curious element of the self-fulfilling prophecy about the planning process. The analysis of LAPS returns was fed back to local authorities. The average of the returns was then used in DHSS Planning Guidelines which in turn were used by many authorities as the basis for their LAPS returns since returns were required at a time when budget plans had not been formulated.

The advent of the Conservative Government in May 1979 with its promised cuts in public spending rendered forward planning even more precarious than it had been previously, and the DHSS scrapped any requirement for a return that year. Despite subsequent suggestions that a modified return will be called for, nothing has yet emanated from the DHSS. This sorry history provides the context of local authority social services planning. It is a context of scepticism about even medium-term planning, and a context in which opportunism becomes the only rational service response. By opportunism I mean the seizing of opportunities for change or development as and when they present themselves rather than as part of a coherent strategy. Thus the retirement of a member of staff or the low occupancy of an establishment may provide the opportunity for change which would not otherwise have ranked as a departmental priority.

Joint financing

Joint financing is an illustration of the application of opportunism in social policy. The achievement of improved collaboration between health and personal social services has been a goal of central government since community care was first adopted as a strategic objective. There has been a growing recognition that there are interdependencies between health care and social services. The discharge of patients from large Victorian asylums requires a concomitant expansion of provision of hostels, group homes, and supported lodgings, which are the responsibility of the social services authority. Quicker turnover of beds in acute wards throws added pressure on domiciliary services like home helps and meals services. Only the DHSS, in its headlong zeal for cuts, failed to recognize this interdependence, with the result that no assessment was made of the impact of cuts in social service provision on health care when Ministers were calling for a 7 per cent reduction in spending. Notwithstanding the odd blemish however joint planning and collaboration has been a consistent strategy.

The joint planning machinery set up in 1974 – Joint Consultative

Committees (JCC) where members of the area health authority meet with local authority members, receiving reports from Joint Care Planning Teams (JCPT) where senior officers of the area health authority meet with local authority senior officers to develop strategy and programming, which in turn receives reports from District Planning Teams in which officers of the health district and local authority representatives meet to plan the development of specific services – is undeniably cumbrous. Proposals can get batted backwards and forwards without clear resolution. The new health authority planning system based on a two-year timetable, and geared to the new health authority structure without area health authorities, may simplify procedures in metropolitan areas. Elsewhere it will complicate matters as county authorities will have several health authorities with which to negotiate.

Joint financing was introduced in 1976 by Barbara Castle, the then Secretary of State for Social Services, specifically as a pump-priming device to oil the wheels of joint planning. It has been a conspicuous success, even allowing for the uncritical enthusiasm of Ministers for whom it has assumed the status of an incantation when they are subject to criticism about the impact of reduced public spending. The aim was to provide health service resources for local authority social services expenditure where this was likely to be of greater benefit in terms of total care. Projects have to be approved by the JCPT and JCC before going to the Area Health Authority itself. Financial support is available for the full cost of the project in the starting-up year but with the local authority assuming full financial responsibility over five or seven years. This tapering-off has become a controversial issue, particularly as local authority expenditure has been increasingly restricted. Successive circulars have added to the flexibility of the scheme, but the essential problem for local authorities remains the requirement to take on additional revenue expenditure in years when their budgets are contracting.

The DHSS refrained from direct instructions on the type of projects to be supported by joint financing. And here the element of opportunism came in. Local authorities were anxious about the revenue impact of joint financing. Local authorities' capital spending had been severely cut by successive spending reductions. And as no DHSS controls existed on the use of joint financing capital monies, many authorities have therefore consciously used joint financing to support their flagging capital programme. In 1979/80 one quarter of all capital spending on social services came from joint financing. The other element of opportunism came in the decision of Directors of Social Services fully to utilize the joint financing allocation while recognizing that it skewed departmental priorities by emphasizing health-related projects. It did offer a prospect of minimal growth while budgets were being cut elsewhere. And by 1981, joint financing represented between 4 per cent and 5 per cent of all personal social services spending, no insignificant amount.

The mentally handicapped have been major beneficiaries of joint financing. The Jay Report (1979) gave an impetus to community care of the mentally handicapped, and joint financing was an obvious vehicle to transfer patients in long-stay hospital care to hostel provision. The recent consultative document *Care in the Community* (DHSS 1981b) offers similar opportunities for Directors of Social Services to utilize health service funds in order to develop resources in the community. The welcome which it has received has however been muted. Local authorities are very conscious of the revenue burden which they will eventually have to assume. Even the proposal to provide 100 per cent joint financing for ten years, effectively deferring full payment by local authorities until the twenty-first century, has not alleviated their suspicions.

While illustrating the continuity in public policy in relation to community care of the elderly, mentally handicapped, and mentally ill over the last twenty years, the true significance of *Care in the Community* (DHSS 1981b) may lie in the variations developed on the theme of transfer of resources from health care to social services. In addition to the proposals on joint financing, there are ingenious devices to attach a sum of money to discharged patients as an incentive to local authorities to provide services and a number of permutations on the joint planning of services.

It is evident that a switch of the scale discussed cannot be brought about without an extension of joint planning between health and social services. More controversial however is the proposal that this might be effected by combining the managerial responsibilities for a client group, thus drawing together all the health and social services resources in an area under one management. While this begs a number of questions – which service provides the management, how are generic social workers to be apportioned, would medical staff accept social services management – it illustrates an important strand of thinking within the DHSS. The future management patterns of social services, and their relationship with the health service structure, are discussed further in the concluding chapter.

Resource management

But if opportunism is a dominant characteristic of social services planning, the economic situation has had a broader impact on policy formation. Webb sums this up as a switch from policy as intent to emphasis on resource management (Webb 1979). In the enthusiasm which followed the advent of new enlarged departments, many Directors sought to encapsulate departmental policy in handbooks or manuals. In one sense this is feasible, for from the centre management can lay down statements such as 'no child shall be received into care solely because of homelessness', but the detailed working out of policy takes place at a very different level. Social workers do exercise considerable decentralized authority in relation to their clients. Webb argues therefore that the policy process consists of three stages: policy intent – the strategic objective; programming – the allocation of resources to this end; and implementation – the operational task of bringing about the necessary administrative and professional activities.

The management of resources has become the language of social services forward planning. In the early seventies, the broad policies of developing a preventive strategy for child care services and building up domiciliary care as an alternative to residential provision were sufficient. Now they would find expression – as indeed they did in the *Priorities* document (DHSS 1976) and its successor, *The Way Forward* (DHSS 1977) – in terms of differential growth rates between service areas. The unfortunate impact of this approach is to divide services on a client group basis, a division which cannot easily be reconciled with the usual organizational pattern of fieldwork and where priorities cannot easily be reflected in the immediate decision-making of fieldworkers.

The view of forward planning presented here is undeniably sceptical. Rational models do however exist. They may work in a few very unusual local authorities, but they are uncharacteristic. The vicissitudes of government policy and the operational imperative of opportunism militate against rational planning. One of the clearest exposi-tions of a rational planning process has been given by Anderson, describing a system in use in Cambridgeshire (Anderson 1979). This deliberately set out to involve practitioners in the exercise of policy formulation. He stresses the relative ignorance of social workers of the process of planning and their reluctance to adhere to the constraints imposed by the rigidities of the timetable for budget preparation.

In Cambridgeshire each division is asked to state its priorities for the ensuing financial year in the spring. They do so against the background of guidelines setting out a timetable for decision-taking, the resource assumptions, and any policy guidance agreed by the social services department. The guidelines are accompanied by an information base outlining centrally held information about the division, its population resources, and services, together with some comparative data about standards of service. The division is then asked to produce a three-year plan including any costed proposals on the basis of existing policy and available resources.

Such an approach in a large county with decentralized services enables each division to determine its own local priorities and to develop a local philosophy of care. It also means that new projects are identified and costed at an early stage of the planning process, and can be introduced after full consultation with all the interest groups affected. Too often the opportunistic approach means that schemes are introduced into a programme without this necessary preliminary work with the result that substantial modification is needed once the scheme begins to operate. Most important, the rationality of the planning process does enable a comparison of existing projects with proposed projects to be undertaken on a value for money basis, and makes the capital programme the servant of forward planning, rather than its arbiter. The demands which the capital programme makes on staffing and the long lead time in bringing projects to fruition mean that a building project can, as has been shown, pre-empt a large slice of available resources. A three-year plan enables Committees clearly to see the looming revenue consequences, and their impact on other desirable projects.

Corporate management

While corporate management was briefly discussed earlier with a suggestion that this approach is vulnerable at a time of limited resources, in theory it offers the best possible way of dealing with such difficulties. It enables the local authority to look at the total range of services and their interrelationships, and to make adjustments where they will do the least harm. The education service has in some areas suffered as a result of the corporate process. Falling school rolls provide a range of options for authorities from making savings in the teacher force wholly proportional to the decline in pupils to utilizing the opportunity to improve the teacher–pupil ratio and educational standards without any reduction in teacher numbers. This choice has been influenced in the direction of the savings option by the powerful impact of the corporate process. Left entirely to departmental decision-making and political influence, the education lobby might have enjoyed more success in improving service standards. Set against the grim reality of service reductions elsewhere, the education service has been obliged to yield to a broader view of priorities.

The mechanism whereby corporate management is reflected in the organizational structure varies greatly between local authorities. Common elements tend to be the free-floating Chief Executive able to take a broad view across departments and not responsible for any service provision, a small group of Chief Officers meeting regularly to agree a corporate strategy, and a powerful Policy and Resources Committee at the pinnacle of the committee structure. Sometimes there is a division between service committees – for instance, housing and social services – and resources committees, which deal with the financial and programming aspects. The committee structure is however essentially a device to legitimate the power relationships which already exist between members, between officers, and between members and officers.

At the top levels of local authority management, one will find an acutely developed political sense with both a small and a large 'P'. Party politics is important. The Chief Officer needs to be aware of feelings within the respective party groups, to recognize particularly sensitive issues, and to reflect as accurately as possible the wishes of the majority group in the policies which he pursues. The ethical and professional issues which this can produce are discussed below in the context of officer–member relationships. For the moment, it is sufficient to note that the Chief Officer who fails to keep closely in touch with opinion in the majority group is unlikely to find counterbalancing support from his colleague Chief Officers. But if a party political awareness is important, so too is a political sense in terms of the distribution of power and influence within the Chief Officers. In most groups, one or two individuals emerge as leaders. They may not formally hold the leadership role, but their influence on decisions is critical. Directors of Social Services are rarely amongst them. The influence which Directors of Social Services exercise may well depend, however, on their relationship with those key individuals.

If the Treasurer is a key figure (and he frequently is), the Director needs to establish swiftly the attitude of the Treasurer to financial control. If the Treasurer regards estimates as sacrosanct, and treats a request for a supplementary estimate as indicative of a failure of management control, the Director may well spend more time on getting financial information than if the Treasurer takes a relaxed view of virement and sees estimates as the total provision for the service area within which adjustments can be made. If the Chief Executive is the key figure, the Director may opt to put more of his energies into corporate planning and strategy (assuming his input would be welcomed) even at the expense of time spent on his own department. In each authority, the judgement has to be made. While the first Chief Executive from a social services background is still awaited, a number of Directors have served as Deputy Chief Executive reflecting their developing role in local authority management.

The Chief Executive of a voluntary organization, or the Chief Probation Officer, has different political problems with which to contend. Voluntary social work agencies produce far more problems of disciplinary proceedings and representation for the British Association of Social Workers than statutory agencies even though the numbers working in these settings are less than a quarter of those in the public sector. One evident reason is the lack of established lines of accountability and clearly recognized procedures for handling disciplinary issues in voluntary agencies. The cumbrous mechanisms of local authorities do serve to deal with many such issues long before they reach flashpoint. Without that protection, the Chief Executive needs highly developed skills in man management. He also needs an effective working relationship with the Chairman of the Management Committee.

Management Committees – like most committees – can be all-powerful or they can be impotent. They can leave all disciplinary issues to paid staff, or they can involve themselves directly. The very nature of their voluntary commitment sometimes seems to provide a moral justification for committee members to go further than would normally be expected in becoming involved in the minutiae of management. For the professional social worker, relationships with a lay committee carry a seed of mutual suspicion and in the context of voluntary agencies it is more difficult to prevent that seed from germinating. It is here that the Chairman–Chief Executive rapport is so important in defining respective roles and responsibilities, and enforcing that definition on recalcitrant committee members. The support and counselling which an experienced Chairman can provide is an inestimable help to the Chief Executive in a voluntary agency, for he lacks the support from colleagues which is available to Chief Officers in the public sector.

Probation management

The position of Chief Probation Officers is also very different from that of their local government colleagues. First, their boundaries are not necessarily coterminous with local authority social services. In metropolitan counties the probation service is organized at county level, but social services at district level. Second, the probation service – although 80 per cent funded by the Home Office – has to rely on officers from outside the service for financial and secretarial input to the Probation Committee, roles often filled by the County Treasurer and County Secretary respectively. The Chief Probation Officer is heavily dependent on the goodwill and co-operation of his colleagues from other settings.

The financial dependence on the Home Office is mirrored by the strong influence which the inspectorate has exercised on professional standards and the evolution of the service – an influence which has been signally absent from the work of the Social Work Service of the DHSS. By controlling promotion to senior posts in the service, and by its influence on training for the service, the Inspectorate's influence has been benign. It represents however a real constraint on the freedom of action of the individual Chief Officer, and is a body whose views have to be taken into account in policy formation.

In both voluntary organizations and in the probation service, the emphasis is very much on annual budgeting. In the former, the uncertainty of grant aid is a factor militating against long-term planning, in the latter the dependence on the Home Office removes any possibility of development financed from other sources. Haxby has suggested a new structure for the service with greater financial powers, possibly admitting the transfer of resources from one part of the penal system to another through the medium of a Community Corrections Board (Haxby 1978). The anomalous position of the service does limit development, but whether the Home Office would be willing fully to devolve responsibility for provision to local boards remains very doubtful.

Programme budgeting

In the years when corporate planning was taken up enthusiastically, programme budgeting was presented as a tool whereby greater efficiency could be achieved throughout the public sector. By using cost benefit analysis, operational research, and systems analysis techniques, it was thought a rational approach could be brought to the budgetary cycle. Similar techniques were applied by the DHSS with the most essential function of the programme budget envisaged as 'a link between, on the one hand, policy formulation and the planning of individual programmes . . . and, on the other, resource planning and . . . decisions about overall strategy' (Banks 1979). In the USA Planning-Programming-Budgeting Systems (PPBS) failed to achieve their original goals. Gorham (1967) has suggested four reasons for this failure. First, a technical problem of lack of data – a familiar difficulty for social service researchers, who, despite having to collect a plethora of statistics, know very little about client views of services. Second was the difficulty in defining the benefits of welfare services in money terms, an essential ingredient of cost-benefit analysis. Third, comparing the benefits of different programmes was conceptually difficult, and fourth, different programmes go to different people. How can the benefits of home help for a socially isolated old man truly be weighed against a day nursery place for a lone parent?

Banks provides an interesting account of the application of programme budgeting in the DHSS (Banks 1979). This was accompanied by departmental reorganization on client group lines and linked to a new planning system, which led to policy statements emanating from each policy branch. Four claims are made for programme budgeting. First, it serves as a tool for linking policies to resources; second, it increases feedback from decisions on policies and priorities to decisions on financial allocations; third, programme budgeting improves manpower planning by ensuring that the priority developments within services are reflected in manpower policies; fourth, it improves linkages between departmental policies and those of local and health authorities. These gains serve as a salutary reminder of how uncoordinated and rudimentary were planning procedures prior to the advent of programme budgeting, but even these gains have now been lost. The latest DHSS statement on policies and priorities, *Care in Action*, contains no reference whatever to the financial relationship implicit in the statement of priorities and makes no attempt to reconcile the priorities set out with resources likely to be available for local authorities. The government itself summarized the deficiencies of programme budgeting in its warning about the validity of cost-benefit analysis expressed in its response to the criticisms of the House of Commons Select Committee on Social Services. 'Such comparisons become more difficult and less reliable the greater the variations in the packages of care delivered, in the needs of the individuals who receive them, and in the outcomes sought' (DHSS 1980: 13).

Member–officer relationships

The focus of this chapter hitherto has been the nature of the planning and budgetary process in local authorities and other social work agencies. The relationships between key figures including Chairmen have been touched upon only in so far as they illuminate that process, but the member–officer relationship warrants further examination as it raises broad issues about the responsibilities of the professional working in a local government context. It also takes a very different form in local government from the probation service, which in turn is different from a voluntary agency, so study of this area also helps to clarify the nature of the distinctive settings for social work practice.

Briefly expressed, the role of the elected members is to determine policy and to allocate resources between service areas, the role of officers is to organize services to fulfil those policies within the resources available. It sounds a simple and clear differentiation of roles. In reality, it is far from that. Officers, because of their expertise, have considerable influence on policy. Chief Officers have considerable influence on resource allocation. Members too can sometimes stray across the policy boundary into matters of procedure and organization. With the effective boundary clear theoretically but blurred in practice tensions inevitably arise.

What is policy? It is not easy to distinguish between the strategic policy, which most would accept is clearly a member responsibility, and operational policy in terms of day-to-day decision-making about priorities. A member who has argued forcefully for expansion of the home help service may find it hard to accept that his elderly mother does not meet the departmental criteria for a home help service. And few things cause greater resentment among social workers than referrals from councillors with an expectation that they will receive quicker and better treatment by virtue of the source of referral.

It is here that interesting ethical issues are raised. If a councillor becomes involved with a family and intervenes on their behalf, how should their interest be handled by the department? If preferential treatment is given the usual priorities on the basis of need are subverted causing anger among other social workers. Yet if the social workers handle the referral in the usual way, the elected member may form an impression that the department is inefficient. The political dimension has to be recognized by social workers. The perception which elected members have of the department, its efficiency and its services, does influence the allocation of resources, and does matter. If a councillor's referral seems to him to have disappeared into the pending tray, or if his queries go unanswered, he is unlikely to make generous assumptions about pressure of work but to be critical of standards of service.

The ideal is clear. Councillors should receive the same treatment as do other members of the public. They should not be able to (nor should they seek) to distort priorities. But like other members of the public, they are entitled to prompt acknowledgement of their enquiries and to be given a clear explanation of the reasons why a service cannot be given immediately. And too often it is this basic courtesy which is denied to clients and councillors alike. If there are valid reasons arising from staff shortages why this reply cannot be given to all clients, there is a case for giving preferential treatment to councillors by way of explaining the problems facing the department.

Members' involvement on behalf of individuals does provide social workers at area level with a chance to educate councillors. Unhappily this harmonious picture does not always apply. Senior managers have a responsibility to their staff to protect them from political pressure, and a number of Directors have clashed with councillors on sensitive issues like access to files.

Another source of tension between officers and members relates to unpalatable decisions. Inevitably cuts are highly sensitive, and a great deal of apocalyptic talk emanates from those most likely to be affected. But the language of priorities is the stock-in-trade of social services management. It is therefore naive to argue as BASW did at the time of its 'Care Costs' campaign that the responsibility for priority decisions was entirely political. BASW's aim was to shift the odium for decisions from social workers, who were in the front line receiving the backlash from clients, to political leadership. Yet professionals do have a responsibility to manage priorities within available resources, and the effective decision, for example, to cut aids rather than staff is likely to be professional rather than political.

If the difficult financial situation and service reductions created initial tensions between members and officers, the situation worsened in many metropolitan areas with the social workers' strike. When a service-giving group strikes for the first time – whether it is doctors, nurses, or social workers – the impact is immense, for not only does such action challenge established patterns of negotiation it also challenges society's moral judgements about vocation and brings a stronger reaction than if industrial action is taken by train drivers, power engineers, or miners. The protracted strikes meant that bitterness increased, attitudes hardened, and relationships between social workers and councillors (and their own management) came under strain. The legacy of that period can be seen in the mutual suspicion evident in areas like Liverpool, where successive issues – access to files, inquiries into assessment centres, staff reductions – are overlain by the history of misunderstanding.

The Report of the Paul Brown Inquiry in the Wirral presented a grim picture of member–officer relationships. The Chairman of the Social Services Committee for two years is described in terms which make him sound every Director's nightmare.

'He assumed a highly eccentric role. He was not merely inter-
ventionist, he interfered in the actual detailed running of the
Department. He made excessive demands on senior management
in the referral of individual cases. He was an aggressive personality
given to dramatic and inappropriate phrases (such as 'heads will
roll') when shortcomings occurred in the Department. Although he
had the interests of the Department at heart his method of working was unpredictable. He would make policy decisions and policy
changes without first considering the implications in depth with the
Director.'   (Brown Report 1980: 103)

The report, with some understatement, concludes that 'his style of
chairmanship helped to undermine the effectiveness of the management and the work of the Department'.

Having described this, the report goes on to consider the role of the
councillor. Again it is worth quoting the relevant paragraph. Councillors' role should be

'that of policy makers having general supervision of the Department. Their role was not to intervene in the professional handling of
individual cases; casework must be left to the professional social
worker. Inevitably the conscientious Councillor will receive requests for help of a welfare nature. It is right that he should assess
those requests and channel them in the right direction. However
there can be . . . such a volume of requests that a Social Services
Department becomes unfairly burdened and pressurised. We feel
that Councillors should exercise a measure of restraint and should
not expect referrals coming through them to receive priority as of
right.'   (Brown Report 1980: 104)

The Brown Report, while much criticized in relation to its main
findings, was obliged to address itself to the issue of member–officer
relationships because of the almost total breakdown which had taken
place. Its conclusion provides authoritative backing for social workers
and managers, and could usefully form the basis for discussion in
areas still experiencing difficulties in achieving a successful working
relationship with local councillors.

In its evidence to the Barclay Inquiry, BASW commented on
the tensions between members and officers, and suggested a number
of ways in which more effective working relationships could be

established. They could be used by senior and middle managers to defuse troubled situations. The six suggestions are:

(1) the establishment of a sub-committee or similar devolved structure involving staff and the local community;
(2) the linking of individual councillors with area officers and specific projects to develop understanding of the range of social services responsibilities;
(3) the linking of social services staff with ward councillors;
(4) the use of induction courses for new councillors and those newly appointed to the social services committee;
(5) the establishment of mixed working groups of councillors, managers, and main grade workers to look at specific issues (a device used with considerable success in Strathclyde);
(6) the development of joint consultative machinery bringing staff and members together (BASW 1981).

The Probation and After-care Service is far less vulnerable than social services departments to officious interference from members of the Committee. This reflects two distinct influences. First, Probation and After-care Committees are not subject to direct election. Members therefore do not have the same sense of authority over the running of the service which Social Services Committees feel as a result of their electoral accountability. Nor are Probation and After-care Committee members subject to the pressures of individual constituents seeking assistance, with the implicit threat of withdrawn electoral support if the assistance is not forthcoming. Second, the tradition of individual responsibility and professional autonomy of the probation service means that Chief Officers are not subject to the same pressure as Directors in relation to individual cases.

The lack of overt political infighting means that Probation and After-care Committees do not contain members 'playing to the gallery' whereas most Social Services Committees contain one or two members who use the public forum to construct headline-catching speeches.

In voluntary organizations, as was discussed earlier, the contact between Chairman and Chief Executive is the vital factor rather than between the Committee of Management as a whole and the Chief Executive. Time has an important bearing on this for an active and committed Chairman is likely to have detailed knowledge of the workings of the organization whereas the contact of other Committee members will be more peripheral.

Citizen participation

Elected members provide the formal means of public participation, but in its advocacy of citizen participation the Seebohm Report expressed a conviction that social services departments needed to go much further if they were to achieve the community-orientated family service which the report envisaged. Four benefits were envisaged from maximum feasible participation of individuals and community groups in the planning, organization, and provision of services. First, this would assist the working out of democratic ideas at local level; second, this would help departments to identify need; third, this would expose defects in services; fourth, it would mobilize new resources. Of these benefits, only the last has been significantly developed at local and national level when the overall shortage of resources has focused political attention on the untapped community resources.

Overriding all these benefits, however, the report argued that the development of citizen participation would reduce the stigma which had been linked with receipt of welfare services since the days of the Poor Law. Self-help groups, foster-care groups, devolvement of management responsibilities in homes to the residents, and encouragement of volunteers were seen as means to promote a participatory climate. One way of stimulating development envisaged in the report was the establishment of 'new forms of bodies' advisory to the area offices, which could discuss community needs and services and which would include consumers and volunteers alongside elected members.

The reality has been far more prosaic. The demand for citizen participation, at its peak immediately following the 1968 disturbances which administered a severe shock to western European governments, has fallen away. While some limited progress has been made, particularly in the use of volunteers, and a positive awareness of the potential contribution of community groups, the gap between those delivering services and the recipients of services remains wide. Where co-options (representing consumer interests) have been made to Social Services Committees, their voice has been muted. In part, this is because the most obvious candidates for co-option represent client group based organizations and thus can contribute only a partisan view to discussions of service priorities.

The move to participation has hit a more fundamental snag. This is the challenge that it poses to the classical view of local government oganization with elected representatives having the responsibility both to articulate the needs and interests of their constituents and to formulate policy. Any participatory model is seen as a threat to this established pattern, yet it is only with the concurrence and support of elected members that the type of advisory body envisaged in the Seebohm Report can function effectively. And consumer participation can be a threat to social services managers. While much of the talk about bureaucracies may represent hyperbole, there is inevitably a defensiveness inherent in large organizations when challenged by unpredictable pressures from outside the organization. To encourage bodies which by definition are likely to be critical of the quality and level of existing provision requires considerable managerial self-confidence.

Enough has been said in this chapter hitherto to demonstrate that planning social services provision cannot be a wholly coherent, rational process working on clearly defined assumptions about resources. The dominant characteristic of the past five years has been the crisis orientation of departments. The crisis of the early 1970s which resulted from the explosive demand growth for service provision has been succeeded by a crisis in which resource assumptions are constantly being modified. This lays a heavy burden upon managers at all levels in social work agencies for long-range planning has become virtually impossible because of this uncertainty.

Senior managers do have to sustain a strategic view of possible developments, for instance the expansion of domiciliary services or the transfer of patients from long-stay hospitals, while acknowledging that the pace of change is uncertain. The priorities may vary too from year to year, depending on resources, political will, staff changes, and other factors, and the selection of priorities will reflect a balance between opportunism and the attainment of strategic objectives. The skills required are numeracy in terms of understanding the possibilities of switching budgetary resources, political sensitivity in working with members, and an awareness of research findings and developments elsewhere which could be translated into the local context.

For middle managers, area officers and team leaders, the requirements of planning are rather different. Their challenge is to develop an understanding of the needs of the local community, and to initiate services which are responsive to those needs. It is suggested that there are ways in which greater involvement of consumers, local organizations, and elected members can be achieved. This requires the manager to raise his head above the grind of coping with referrals and ensuring that individuals receive an adequate level of service to the broader issues of social need. One way of achieving this dual perspective has been discussed (Currie and Parrott 1981). It is the core role of the middle manager to ensure that policy formation is informed by the social needs uncovered in practice, and that practice in turn is responsive to those needs.

The view outlined above may best be clarified by an example, an example deliberately chosen from an area hitherto relatively neglected by social work agencies despite their extensive knowledge of its implications – unemployment. Senior management has to take a view of the impact of unemployment on the area and the services offered. This view would be influenced by geography – whether unemployment was a temporary phenomenon as perhaps in the south-east England, or a long-term problem as in Merseyside and Scotland – by politics, for the political complexion of the area influences the readiness of elected members to incur expenditure on projects to combat unemployment, and by any research findings on correlations between unemployment and social stress, delinquency or psychiatric problems. Middle managers would influence this judgement by their assessment of the impact of unemployment on their workload, and by suggested responses.

Assuming that the political will existed, a range of responses could come from this interaction – training workshops supported by Manpower Services Commission funds, drop-in centres, specialized counselling services, and extensive Youth Opportunity employment schemes in day centres and residential homes. But the process by which these projects develop would be the interaction between policy, planning, and practice – an interaction which management has to stimulate and sustain.

8

Style and skills

What makes a good manager? One can find many definitions of management itself, but few are able to prescribe the characteristics required of a good manager. The manager has to fulfil many roles. Some have already been discussed in earlier chapters – supervision, planning, budgeting, and allocation of resources – and other roles will be considered. The multi-faceted demands on management make it almost impossible for any individual to be universally regarded as a good and effective manager, for frequently concern for people and staff and concern for efficiency and attainment of goals (both inherently desirable) will be in conflict. It is how that always latent conflict is handled which influences staff perception of managers.

Social work agencies have no established house style of management. Unlike the Civil Service with its established promotion patterns and sophisticated in-service training, there is no ready-made route to the Director's desk for aspiring CQSW students. The Association of Directors of Social Services has struggled to define even minimum qualifications for appointment, so disparate are the experiences of its members. It is therefore worth looking at management style and its impact on social work practice to see if there is a style peculiarly fitted to the social work context.

The classical definition of management advanced by Fayol in 1916 identified five managerial functions – planning, organizing, co-ordinating, commanding, and controlling. These, however, more accurately describe the goals of management than the actual day-to-day process of management, and have subsequently been refined.

Theories of leadership

TRAIT THEORIES

Three basic theories of leadership have emerged, which can be categorized as relating respectively to managerial characteristics, management style, and situational analysis. The first theory looks at leadership in terms of the traits of the ideal leader – intelligence, self-assurance, decision-making powers, initiative, and effectiveness. If all leaders had the drive and entrepreneurial flair of Sir Michael Edwardes or Lord Weinstock, the country's economy would immediately benefit from improved management, is the popular expression of trait theory. It views the world as something which can be changed by leadership alone – a view widely held by directors of football clubs.

STYLES OF LEADERSHIP

The second theory views leadership in terms of managerial styles. The participative manager leaning to a democratic style is widely preferred to the autocratic one, yet there is no conclusive evidence that a participative approach is more effective in terms of productivity or the achievement of goals. Some of these issues are discussed in the managerial grid, a behavioural concept widely used in management training (Blake and Mouton 1964). This characterizes managerial styles on a grid with two dimensions – a concern for people, and a concern for production (or achievement of goals in a social work context). Managers are ranked on a nine-point scale according to their responses to various tests. The ideal manager in the terms of the grid is a 9:9 manager, one who combines a high level of concern for people with a concern for achieving goals and who sees no irreconcilable conflict between the two.

SITUATIONAL THEORIES

If the trait theories exemplify a belief that leaders are born rather than made, the management style approach assumes a capacity for modification. The third approach examines situational theories where the effectiveness of a style, or an individual leader, depends on the components of the situation. Churchill was a great war leader but was ineffective in peace-time, is a popular representation of a situational analysis of leadership. The ability of the manager to control his environment is an important feature of this analysis, which sees the use of powers of reward and coercion as tools at the disposal of the manager.

Applying these theories of leadership to a social work context focuses attention on the conceptual confusion which exists within social work about leadership and management. In most organiz-ations, and certainly in those like many social work agencies where the combination of reduced resources and public criticism have sapped morale, there is a yearning for strong decisive leadership. Yet at the same time there is profound ambivalence about the impli-cations of that leadership style in a department where the dominant values are those of social work, with its orientation towards the sharing of problems through unhurried discussion and acting at a pace acceptable to all involved. As a consequence there is a tendency in social work agencies to govern by consensus. Yet even in organiz-ations where the staff share a common training and have similar roles – a university or school – there are acute difficulties in reconciling effective decision-making with consensus. In an agency like a social services or probation department with a range of staff from different disciplines working in different settings, consensus can rarely be achieved and if widely sought can lead to lengthy delays in reaching decisions.

This chapter cannot offer a prescription for effective management in the sense of defining the characteristics and style of good managers. What it can do is to proceed negatively by identifying the nature of managerial work and the various roles which managers are required to play, and hence to appreciate the failure of certain management styles fully to take into account the complexity of the task. There are two major sources of information in examining the nature of manage-rial work. Mintzberg (1973) has written a major text on management theory generally, but in the context of social work Project INNISS (Streatfield and Wilson 1980) has interesting findings which com-plement those of Mintzberg and suggest that the demands of manage-ment in social work are less different from management elsewhere than is sometimes argued.

Characteristics of managerial work

The main characteristics found by Mintzberg (1973) in studying managerial work were brevity, variety, and fragmentation. Most contacts, phone calls, and enquiries were short. The range of work was wide. The pattern was fragmented with major strategic issues and the relatively trivial mixed up throughout the managerial day. These characteristics of the work contain a threat in themselves to effective performance, because they make it difficult for the manager to keep a focus on broad general issues and encourage him to become preoccupied with specifics. The pressure encourages an orientation to action, with mail which requires an immediate response being given priority over major documented reports. The largest slice of management time goes in scheduled meetings, which allow formal contacts over a longer duration to deal with a prescribed agenda or a particular issue. Unsurprisingly, Mintzberg found that managers of public sector organizations spent more time in scheduled meetings than managers in commercial and industrial settings.

Project INNISS was designed to identify and clarify the needs of social services departments for information, and to examine the nature of information transactions within agencies. Three-fifths of information exchanges were oral, most usually face to face, with just under a third involving reading or writing. Senior managers spent nearly half their working week in scheduled meetings, with the proportion decreasing down the line management hierarchy, to social workers who spent less than 10 per cent of their working week in meetings. Information was found to flow upwards to top management as described in departmental management charts, but difficulties were experienced in communicating downwards through the hierarchy. The volume of paperwork meant that items for senior managers rarely received more than an attention period of three minutes. Mintzberg's characteristics of brevity, variety, and fragmentation were clearly present.

While handling information is an important aspect of management, there are other aspects which warrant consideration, particularly those dealing with interpersonal relationships and those dealing with the decision-making characteristics of management. Mintzberg suggests that there are ten observable roles which come together in management. Each of these can also be seen in a social work context.

They are:

(a) *Figurehead:* The manager has to carry out some social and legal duties by virtue of his status. These may range from the insignificant – presenting a leaving gift to a junior member of the staff – to formal – the promulgation of new agency policy – but rest with the manager because of the symbolic nature of his position. Outside bodies may also use the manager in this way to safeguard and assert their own status.

(b) *Leader:* The manager's relationship with his subordinates is an important element in his overall effectiveness. He is responsible for hiring, training, and promoting them, for motivating them, and for defining their tasks. While the leader of a social work agency is subject to constraints as in any organization the ability of a Director or Chief Officer to motivate staff has a marked impact on morale.

(c) *Liaison:* The manager has a network of contacts outside the organization on which he can draw. While these may flow from his figurehead role initially, they are often developed in ways which yield significant benefits to the agency. A Chief Officer may use the contacts which he has with local universities to encourage research projects which are helpful to the agency, or stimulate local industrialists to be sympathetic to the employment problems of youngsters in care or ex-offenders.

(d) *Monitor:* The manager has to have a thorough understanding of the organization. He needs to have regular and reliable sources of information in order to be able to assess the success of the agency in meeting its objectives. While some of that feedback will be documented, the manager has also to assess the validity of verbal impressionistic evidence passed to him by subordinates. By monitoring, the manager is able to identify necessary changes.

(e) *Disseminator:* The manager not only receives information on his monitoring and liaison capacities, he has also the task of feeding this back into the organization if he wishes to modify policies and procedures. The problem of delegation is bound up with the issue of dissemination. By virtue of his central position in the agency, the manager is often best placed to take decisions but is unable to do so without overloading himself with responsibilities. The supervisory relationship exemplifies this dilemma when the supervisor has consciously to hold back and allow practitioners to take their own decisions, albeit with the supervisor disseminating as much information and knowledge as he can.

(f) *Spokesman:* The role of spokesman is close to that of figurehead, but in this instance reflects a genuine attribution of expertise and knowledge to the manager rather than the symbolic leadership role of the figurehead. For managers in social work agencies, the spokesman role can be important in dealings with the press and outside bodies. The success of the manager in the spokesman role will depend on his possession of the necessary authority and information. The Chief Officer's contacts with the Committee reflect this public relations aspect of his work.

(g) *Entrepreneur:* This role goes further than the entrepreneurial function in commercial management. It describes the manager's ability to initiate and control the pace and direction of change, and his role in identifying areas of the organization which require improvement. Bringing about change can involve the manager in delegation. Directors are obliged to pass responsibility for specific projects to senior managers to avoid overload.

(h) *Disturbance handler:* The aspect of conflict in organizations arising from personality clashes or industrial relations problems is one which managers are obliged to handle. The role is forced on them in part by their figurehead status, in part by their responsibility for affecting change in the environment. The reasons for conflict will be explored in more detail later, but it should be noted that it can be the direct result of innovative entrepreneurial activities. Examples in social work are legion. The change of use of a residential home, or the switch of resources from residential to domiciliary, can trigger complex trade union negotiations and potential arenas of conflict.

(i) *Resource allocator:* The control of organizational resources is vested in the manager. These include both financial and staffing resources. Mintzberg points out that the way in which the manager organizes his own time is an implicit statement of priorities, for his support is required to shift existing organizational priorities. In social work agencies major strategic decisions are likely to be linked to the annual budgetary cycle in which the Chief Officer will be closely involved. The use of overall staff resources will also be an issue reserved for senior level, but some resource issues –

use of small sums of money for preventive work or the use of individual workers' time – will be clearly delegated to local level for decision.

(j) *Negotiator:* The manager is cast in a negotiating role in relation to other agencies. In this capacity he has to discharge also figure-head, spokesman, and resource allocator roles. An example is the participation of the Director of Social Services in a Joint Care Planning Team with the health authority. He is there as a figurehead reflecting the status accorded to joint planning, as spokesman for the policies and procedures of the department, as resource allocator (and entrepreneur) in considering projects for joint financing support, and as negotiator with the health service in working out respective financial allocations for joint care activities.

Social work as antithetic to management

There are elements in social work practice which make the progression to managerial roles peculiarly difficult. First, social workers are taught to individualize problems and have therefore an inherent resistance to the generalizations and aggregation demanded of management; second, social workers' belief in the uniqueness of each individual and his capacity for change promotes resistance to any mechanistic approach to policy development – a corollary of this being an ever-present readiness to challenge agency policies where they bear heavily upon an individual client; third, the emphasis, still prevalent although no longer universal, on psychological and emotional factors militates against examination of the structural factors which need to be worked with; fourth, the democratic orientation of social work means that there is often ambivalence about a move to management; and fifth, the existing promotion patterns in social work remove managers from day-to-day practice, their original motivation for coming into social work.

In the conceptualization of the managerial grid, social workers are likely by virtue of their training to be 1:9 managers with a strong concern for people but with little interest in performance or effectiveness. Their training and orientation are likely to inculcate suspicion of leadership. My own first experience of this was a group discussion of applicants for probation training when eight persons were seated and invited to discuss capital punishment, watched by three silent observers. Even at that fledgling stage, it was not difficult to see that the self-appointed group leader who pronounced his own views dogmatically was unlikely to be accepted for training – subsequent evidence suggested that acceptance bore an inverse relationship to one's contribution to the group discussion. Later group-work theory derived from Bion's (1961) analysis reinforced suspicion of those who bid for leadership roles in groups.

Growth of conflict

This ambivalent attitude to leadership has made the handling of conflict a painful experience for many social work managers. Trained and experienced in coping with aggressive responses from clients, they nevertheless find it difficult to accept (or to understand) similar responses from members of the same professional community. Yet the last decade has seen a new militancy among local authority and public sector workers with social workers often in the van in forcing their unions to take up more overtly political stances. For better or worse, the time has passed when social work managers could rely on professional loyalties to avoid conflict.

Of all the factors which have played a part in the development of conflict in social work agencies, the most influential has to be the impact of public expenditure constraints. The growth, and expectation of continuing growth, in social welfare provision was first slowed, then halted, and has now been reversed as the economic situation has worsened. The revolution in attitudes which this has demanded of management and staff can scarcely be overestimated. For professionals with a sense of commitment to clients' welfare, and with an acute awareness of the problems experienced by their clients (problems compounded by rising unemployment, restrictions on social security payments, and public hostility to 'scroungers'), the change of gear has been particularly painful. It has raised two related issues for social work: first, the ethical responsibility of social workers for clients' welfare and whether this can be wholly discharged by reference to agency policy and restrictions if this involves withdrawal or curtailment of a necessary service; and second, a heightened awareness of the relevance of structural factors in determining the life chances of social services clients, and hence a greater readiness to assert direct political involvement as a social work responsibility. These issues have been compounded by the twin impact of demography and economic problems on social services referrals, which have continued to increase sharply at a time when staff numbers are being cut back. All this has to be seen in the context of a general decline in labour relations in the public sector, and the growing role of trade unions.

The growth of trade unions may be more a reflection of the labour relations climate than the cause, but it is a reality with which social work managers have to deal. In the last fifteen years, NALGO's membership has doubled, NUPE and COHSE have trebled in membership. This is in part the result of a shift in patterns of employment from the manufacturing industry to the service sector, and an increase in the numbers employed by the public sector. The industrial relations conflicts of the early seventies provided a further stimulus to trade union recruitment as legislation like the Employment Protection Act (1974) and Health and Safety at Work Act (1974) increased the power of the trade union movement in the work-place.

Local government historically has been barren ground for trade union activists. The sense of public service is real. The belief in political impartiality is widely held. And in the context of social work, the ethical commitment to clients militates against any action likely to result in a withdrawal or reduction of services. Yet the growth of conflict in social work agencies has been a signal feature of agencies in the latter half of the 1970s with the social work press dominated by strikes, protests, disputes, and confrontations.

Impact of bureaucracy

The impact of bureaucracy is frequently blamed for this worsening climate. Large organizations are bureaucratic in the sense of being governed by rules and procedures. They have to be in order to function effectively. The latent conflict between bureaucracy and professional autonomy has been discussed earlier. What is here significant is the perception held by social workers of the oppressive weight of bureaucracy. This perception is influenced by the number of levels of management between social workers and the Chief Officer, by the number of advisers and non-line managerial staff employed, and by a limited comprehension of the requirements of public accountability. It contributes, however, to a sense of remoteness and distance which provides fertile soil for misunderstandings of management motives for particular actions.

The rules by which the bureaucracy operates are sometimes not made explicit. Social workers have been suspended for placements in breach of departmental policy in relation to child care, where the policy had either not been written down or had not been promulgated to all staff. Few agencies have a comprehensive and up-to-date manual of policy and procedures, yet there is a departmental perception which can be acquired only by experience. This creates a sense of insecurity in practitioners, who cannot be confident that the agency would support them in the event of any mistaken judgements.

The nature of social work practice has changed in social services departments. Of the total workload coming to the department only a minority of cases require the traditional skills of social work and the use of interpersonal relationships. The rest involve advocacy, welfare rights advice, referrals to other agencies, and practical help of various kinds. The preoccupation with following laid-down procedures and completing the appropriate form contributes to an element of routinization in daily work which can increase feelings of alienation.

The reorganization of local government in 1974, following so closely on social services reorganization, created widespread tensions and uncertainty. The jockeying for position, the adaptation to new methods of working, and the inevitable confusion left some staff aggrieved. After a period of relative organizational stability, the pressure to find savings has led a number of departments to undertake restructurings with a consequent reduction of managerial and administrative posts. Each change has to be negotiated; each change creates some dissatisfied staff; each change has potential for conflict.

Yet the development of conflicts often took social work managements by surprise. There were rarely formal channels of communication in existence within social services departments. Interestingly, the probation and after-care service has gone much further in the establishment of consultative machinery, which has helped to limit conflict in the service despite the increasingly militant stance of the National Association of Probation Officers. Management needs to be aware of the official union position, but also to recognize unofficial sources of power. Formal recognition of shop stewards in departments and regular meetings between senior managers and union officials, not only to deal with crisis, are minimum conditions for effective communication.

Handling conflict

The manager's role is, in Mintzberg's terminology, as a disturbance handler. His task is to avoid conflict wherever possible and to minimize it where it is unavoidable, and to manage conflicts in such a way as to minimize the disorder caused. The process of managing conflict therefore needs to be examined.

The first task is to ensure that adequate channels of communication exist for both formal and informal communication between staff and management. In the highly unionized public sector this will almost invariably be with official union representatives. Ease of communication will be improved if regular meetings are held as a matter of routine as was suggested above. This enables the meetings to act in a fire-fighting role to limit damage rather than being themselves the arena in which the conflict is escalated. In any formal meeting the opportunity to explore solutions is likely to be limited, so it is essential to complement formal communication by informal contact in which 'without prejudice' negotiations can take place. Such negotiating conventions need to be clear to both sides if subsequent misunderstandings are to be avoided, but can provide an invaluable means of breaking through an apparent deadlock.

It is important for management to clarify the key negotiating issue. In the social workers' dispute, the right to local negotiations was the formal issue in dispute. In reality, the salary levels of social workers were at the nub of the grievance. After a long period of confusion in which the employers' side attempted to deal with the issue of pay while ignoring local negotiations, an eventual settlement was reached on the basis of local applications of a national framework. This meant that a salary ceiling was effectively imposed with local authorities free to negotiate how to apply the proposed three levels within that. It was a clever negotiating tactic to link the two issues in one offer – but one that could have been made at an earlier stage of the dispute.

The social workers' dispute was unusual in that it arose as a result of an initiative on the trade union side. It should be recognized that in the great majority of disputes, trade unions are reacting to management initiatives and proposals. Closures, changes of use of establishments, reducing posts, freezing vacancies, suspensions, demotions, and restructurings are the characteristic issues which spark off conflict – and each follows from a management decision. What is vital therefore is anticipation of the industrial relations dimension to any managerial actions. Too often social services managements have given the impression of being taken by surprise by the existence of fierce opposition to their reasoned actions. It is not unrealistic to require management to inform/consult/discuss/negotiate with the union if it proposes to make changes which will affect the position of any member of staff in relation to their conditions of work. The nature of that process is deliberately expressed as inform/consult/discuss/negotiate, for it has to be a continuum where the form of contact is dependent on the scale and significance of the changes proposed.

There are two aspects to the process of consultation. First, it has to be genuine with a readiness on the part of management to modify (and in exceptional instances, to withdraw) its proposals to reflect the comments of the union side. Second, it has to be allowed sufficient time for the union members affected to discuss the matter with their representatives. Management time is scarce, and the timescale of decision-making is tight. The lengthy process of consultation is undeniably irritating and inefficient. It is however a necessary condition for achieving harmonious industrial relations, and thus minimizing conflict.

An example of industrial strife

Despite effective structures, genuine consultation, and sensitive management, conflicts will continue. A topical illustration may help to identify the limited responses available to management. Confronted for example with union demands to abandon the proposed closure of a children's home, what options are open to management? First, the management should have given advance warning to the union that this course was to be recommended to Committee, and thus have provided the union with the opportunity to make representations to councillors. Second, the case for closure should be clearly set out, with proposals for the children currently cared for (who should also be informed of possible closure at as early a stage as possible) and those who would otherwise have been placed there, proposals for the redeployment of staff, and the proposed timescale of closure. Third. management should make clear its readiness to be flexible on time-tabling and redeployment but its inability to compromise on the issue of closure.

Contrary to some fantasies, trade unions operate in the real world with a highly developed awareness of the constraints to which managements are subject. If the closure can be justified as inevitable, bearing in mind financial pressures and occupancy levels, the issue may well turn into a search for a safeguarding of the interests of staff members, and thus switch from one where management's room for manoeuvre is nil to one where it has already indicated a readiness to be flexible. The importance of directing attention to areas where there is scope for flexibility is a basic negotiating skill. Just as social workers look for opportunities for movement with clients and sometimes leave intractable areas to concentrate on issues offering potential for change, so too negotiators need to look for areas where flexibility is possible.

If, however, the union refuses to accept the closure and threatens a strike, management has to respond differently. It will need contingency plans in case a strike goes ahead, but in formulating the plans it has to avoid actions which will further antagonize the union leadership. The exercise is one of limiting the damage to the children involved, to the staff, and to management–union relationships. It is vital therefore at all stages of a dispute to keep in contact with the union side even if formally relations have broken down. Unless the dispute has so embittered relationships that attempts will be made to subvert contingency plans, it is sometimes helpful to let the unions know precisely the actions that are to be taken. This helps to dispel the fantasies which are the enemy of rationality in conflict situations.

While there are attractions to elected members and to management in showing that 'business as usual' prevails and to keep services running albeit at a reduced level, it may not be the best course. First, it hardens union resistance. Second, it places invidious pressure on remaining staff to collaborate with management, and third, it is dishonest to pretend that services are unaffected – and that dishonesty can have a political price. The aftermath of the social workers' dispute shows how easy it is to secure political support for reducing the numbers of staff when those staff have been on strike for several months without visible public impact. Closure of a service does dramatize the dispute, and can speed a solution by quickening the will of both sides for a settlement.

Disciplinary proceedings

One potential source of conflict is disciplinary proceedings. The rapid increase in the load of this kind of work undertaken by BASW led the Association to establish a separate Advice and Representation Fund to finance the service required by members. When responsible for this area of work, I was constantly astonished by how few senior managers seemed to be aware of their local authority's disciplinary procedures. Suspensions were imposed when final warnings would have been appropriate, final warnings were issued without first warnings, opportunities of representations had been denied, yet not as part of a Machiavellian plan to deny the rights of employees but rather as a result of confusion and ignorance. There are enough pitfalls when one is familiar with disciplinary procedures without converting the risk of error into a certainty.

Local authority employees – and probation and after-care service employees effectively come under this heading in respect of service conditions – are a privileged class. Their employing authorities are model employers, obliged to meet all the requirements of good practice to a greater degree than many industrial or commercial undertakings. They therefore have established procedures whereby employees can raise a grievance and secure an adequate response, and disciplinary procedures which protect the employee from hasty or ill-judged actions by supervisory staff. While there are minor variations between authorities such procedures provide a framework of informal warning, written warning, final warning, and dismissal, except in cases of gross misconduct where the earlier stages of the process can be leapfrogged. Usually an appeal can be made against each stage of the procedure, to the Chief Officer or to a members' panel.

Managers have to adhere scrupulously to these procedures if they are to succeed in disciplinary action. They have to allow adequate time for the employee to seek representation and prepare his case, and allow him to be represented at the hearing. This quasi-judicial character to disciplinary procedures causes profound unease to many managers, and leads them to avoid such action wherever possible.

The result is that where action is taken, it is frequently after a long history of incapacity or misconduct rather than as an initial step in disciplinary procedures in the hope that the employee's level of performance will improve.

The Chief Officer is often confronted with an invidious situation in disciplinary hearings. A senior manager will have approved the initiation of action, and may have been involved in the preparation of the case against the employee. By finding in favour of the employee, the Chief Officer not only is implicitly criticizing his managerial colleagues but he is also creating a difficult working environment, for the employee may feel free to continue the behaviour or attitudes which created the initial problem.

Those working in voluntary organizations are less likely to enjoy clearly defined disciplinary procedures. In such circumstances, managers have a particular responsibility to ensure that they adhere to the requirements of natural justice and that the nature and purpose of proceedings is clearly explained. Voluntary organizations are less able to 'carry' staff who are not functioning properly than are the larger statutory agencies, but financial considerations have to be subordinate to those of fairness in determining action to be taken. The loyalty and shared commitment of staff in many voluntary organizations makes disciplinary action particularly painful, and other options may be available.

The disciplinary process, partly as a result of adherence to good practice and partly as a result of the split responsibilities of officers and members, can be extremely protracted. Like marriage, it is not to be entered upon lightly and like marriage, it rarely goes smoothly. Other courses are therefore very much more attractive to managers. 'Counselling out' is a euphemistic description of the process used in social work courses with students who are palpably unsuitable, and counselling out can be an appropriate stance for management. It is necessary however to avoid the trap of 'constructive' dismissal where the resignation of a staff member is deemed to have been rendered inevitable as a result of managerial actions. In such circumstances, an appeal can be made to an industrial tribunal. Where disciplinary proceedings go wrong it is often the result of a hasty decision without full consideration of all the possible consequences.

Decision-taking

Decision-taking is central to the management task at all levels. An analytical approach to decision-taking, using the management techniques of the repertory grid, judgement analysis, and decision analysis, can be a useful tool to avoid precipitate decisions.

REPERTORY GRID

The repertory grid developed by Kelly and others (Kelly 1974) is an approach which looks at issues in terms of the options available to management and the criteria which are important to the service. In the jargon of the concept, the various options are described as *elements*, the various criteria as *constructs*. If, for example, the issue to be determined relates to cuts in service provision, the elements might include closures of specific establishments, increased charges for services, reductions in staffing levels, reduced expenditure on Section 1 payments, etc. Defining the criteria which govern the eventual decision is more difficult. They are rarely made explicit except as retrospective rationalization – indeed the capacity to justify the decision retrospectively might be a significant criterion with cynical Chief Officers. In relation to cuts, however, the degree of harm to clients, political acceptability, impact on priority groups, effect on take-up, trade union resistance, etc., are more likely to be significant.

JUDGEMENT ANALYSIS

Having defined the options and the criteria relevant to the decision, the possibility of testing each option against those criteria and thus arriving at a rational decision begins to open up. This involves the use of judgement analysis – a deceptively simple technique (Algie, Hey, and Mallen 1981). It consists of looking at each option and comparing it in turn with each other option against the criteria which have been previously identified. A numerical weighting is given to the degree by which one option is preferred to the other.

Taking an example from the options in relation to cuts may help to clarify the process. If the first three options to be considered are closure of a children's home, cuts in home help service, and not filling vacant posts, and the criterion to be tested is political acceptability, the closure would be ranked against home help cuts on a 1–9 scale with 1 indicating a broad balance between the two options in terms of political acceptability and 9 a total dominance of one option. Thus ranking the closure against the cuts in home care might, in an authority preoccupied by demographic pressures and with little pressure on its child care services, mean that the closure ranked highly for acceptability; closure of an establishment might however be less acceptable than the non-filling of vacant posts. A ranking order on that criterion has thus been established, with non-filling of vacant posts highest in terms of political acceptability and cuts in the home help service lowest. Other criteria relevant to cuts – impact on clients, trade union opposition, speed of bringing about savings – would lead to different rank orders. By giving a numerical value to the relationship between options on each criteria, it is possible with the help of a computer program to arrive at a ranking order for the options against all the relevant criteria. Judgement analysis can also be used on the criteria which, although all relevant, will also have differing degrees of importance.

What has been described may sound complex, but is quite a simple exercise once the options and the criteria have been made explicit. It obliges managers to think rather than act on hunches, and helps them to clarify exactly why particular decisions are being made. It does not relieve management of its ultimate responsibility, but it does provide a conceptual tool to help in analysis of decisions.

DECISION ANALYSIS

The most sophisticated application of this approach is decision analysis. Phillips argues that this usually involves ten steps:

(a) *Recognition that a decision problem exists:* This sounds deceptively simple but is often ignored until a relatively advanced stage under the guise of collecting more information, or undertaking further research.

(b) *Structuring the decision problem:* This involves drawing a decision tree. An example is given below (*Figure 8(1)*) based on the cuts hypothesis discussed above where the decision problem is where to make budget cuts. Decision points are shown as a square, uncertainties with a circle. One major uncertainty for the cuts options is the strength of trade union and staff oppositions. This has been shown on the tree, which is much simplified for the purpose of this example. Nevertheless six possible outcomes are shown dependent on the selected option and the strength of opposition to the proposals.

Figure 8(1) A decision tree

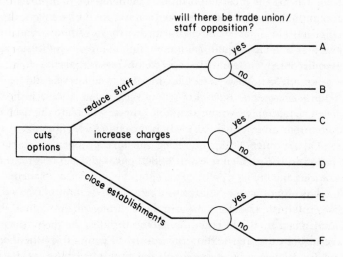

will there be trade union / staff opposition?

(c) *Description of the consequence:* Having a diagrammatic represen-tation of the events, usually with more uncertainties interposed than shown here, it is possible to consider the implications of each route.

(d) *Definition of the criteria:* What makes one outcome more satisfactory than another? It is important to recognize that there are several criteria of utility – speed of savings, least impact on clients, and political acceptability in the cuts example – which may have different degrees of importance according to the political and financial context.

(e) *Evaluation of the consequences for each criterion:* Using a scale from 0 as the worst consequence to 100 as the best, the six outcomes identified can be scored against each criteria. This process is not dissimilar to that employed in judgement analysis. Thus against the speed of savings criterion, trade union and staff opposition might well delay the savings, reductions in staff take time to

achieve, and closure of establishments require a running down
period. D might therefore rank 100, B 80, F 60, C 40, A 20, and E
0. Different rank orders would apply on other criteria.

(f) *Assessment of weightings for each criterion:* If the cuts are required in
the middle of a financial year to prevent the Secretary of State for
the Environment withholding rate support grant, speed of savings will be the most important. If the Director is hoping to be
appointed Chief Executive, political acceptability might rank
highest; if his social work instincts are to the fore, the avoidance of
harm to clients would dominate. But relative weightings are
required. Let us assume that speed of savings is ranked as twice as
important as the other criteria which are of equal weight.

(g) *Determination of the value of outcomes:* With six possible outcomes,
each weighed against the available criteria which are themselves
weighted, a numerical value can be given to each outcome.

Taking outcome A, the rating can be multiplied by the criterion weight, which is taken hypothetically as 0.5 for speed of
savings and 0.25 for political acceptability and harm to clients.

Thus for outcome A, a rating of 20 would be multiplied by 0.5
to equal 10, and for outcome D, a rating of 100 would be
multiplied by 0.5 to equal 50. Going through the possible outcomes in turn, and adding the numerical values from the three
scales applied as in section (e) and multiplied by the criteria
weighting, a figure can be reached for each outcome.

(h) *Assessment of probabilities:* On the example shown, only one uncertainty – that of trade union and staff opposition – was noted. Real
life decision problems often have three or four. For each uncertainty, the possibilities can be weighted. Each cut option is likely
to bring opposition, but it will be strongest where staff interests
are directly challenged by staff reductions or establishment
closures. Charges, however, might have only a 40 per cent
likelihood of staff opposition, and would be accorded a weighting
of 0.4. Closures might have a 90 per cent likelihood of opposition
and staff reductions a 100 per cent certainty, with respective
weightings of 0.9 and 1.

(i) *Application of the weightings:* There now exists a numerical
framework to calculate the available options. By weighting consequences, criteria, and probabilities, an exact calculation can be
made which reflects the uncertainties involved. A high possibility

of vigorous staff and trade union opposition would thus be reflected in the weightings.

(j) *Sensitivity analysis:* Reaching a numerical assessment is not quite the end of the process. Of the various judgements and rankings made throughout the process, there will be some which can be predicted with greater certainty than others. It may be that hard evidence is available – a NALGO policy not to cover for vacant posts if management freeze vacancies, for example – in some instances, but not elsewhere. Where there is uncertainty, the weightings can be changed and the calculation reworked to test how influential was that particular weighting – and thus how confident one can be in the final ranking order.

No great claims are made for the process. 'It serves as an aid to problem solving, as a guide to the decision maker, not as an optional model that dictates the "best" solution to a problem' (Phillips 1980). The language, the mathematical techniques employed, and the potential for modelling and computerizing decision trees are alien to social workers, but are peculiarly well suited to the complex and shifting arena in which many social work decisions and resource decisions have to be taken. While few will wish overnight to adopt such a radical new approach, the modelling techniques which have been described are likely to assume increasing importance in social services planning.

The purpose of this chapter has been to combat a widely held view that social services management is different from management in other settings, that its managers have different training needs, and deploy wholly different techniques. By looking at theories of leadership and the characteristics of managerial work, the substantial overlap between the roles of social work managers and those elsewhere has been demonstrated. Finally, the enormous potential of computerization and modelling as tools to assist managers has been considered in the context of social services applications.

9

The challenge to management

Earlier chapters have considered different aspects of the manager's role in social work agencies. Both those elements which are shared with managers in other settings and those which are peculiar to social work, notably the nature of supervision of practice, have been discussed. The complexity of the management task has been conveyed. In this concluding chapter, four important areas are considered in which social work managements face a major challenge to their resourcefulness and imagination. These are: (1) a growing concern with the effectiveness of social work intervention; (2) the likelihood of severely limited resources; (3) the various patterns of service provision under consideration; (4) the basic challenge to the necessity for management in social work agencies, which finds expression in a yearning for alternative structures.

Effectiveness

Social work managers at all levels are having to cope with a change in orientation from a preoccupation with inputs – staffing, training, finance – to an emphasis on outputs – the effectiveness of social work intervention. Tools for the measurement of effectiveness are insufficiently developed, but a preoccupation with their development can already be seen in some academic circles (B. Davies and Knapp 1978; Sheldon 1978; B. Davies 1981; Ferlie and Judge 1981). When they are fully available, it is likely that some ideas of service delivery will have to be rethought. Goldberg for example has questioned 'the wisdom of closing within the intake phase, as "low priority", those family cases whose problems are not as yet very severe. It may prove more effective in the long run to reverse this policy and to limit the resources which are at present poured into the chronically disorganised families and to spend more casework resources on work with families who have not as yet become severely disrupted' (Goldberg 1978).

Linked to the search for indicators of effectiveness is the trend to more specific identification of objectives, in both training and social work practice. CSS training with its requirement of task analysis and precise learning objectives has been a major factor in changing attitudes. In practice, the search for measures of effectiveness has increased the behaviourist influence. Fischer in the USA, and Mcauley, Sheldon, and Hudson in Britain have questioned the validity of traditional approaches and offered guidance about the application of behavioural techniques in practice (Hudson 1975, 1978; Fischer 1976; Sheldon 1978; R. Mcauley and P. Mcauley 1980; P. Mcauley 1981). The growing adoption of formalized review systems, described in detail in earlier chapters, places a premium on clarity in defining objectives as a means of sharpening up assessments.

This emphasis on empirical validation is new to social work. It has yet fully to influence training courses, has had some influence on practice, but has had very little influence on managers. In their disturbing study of social workers' responses to children made the subject of care orders following offences, Giller and Morris suggest that social workers respond in an intuitive way to the difficulties presented by their clients with theoretical justifications following in the wake of intuition (Giller and Morris 1981). Similarly, social work managers also tend to respond intuitively with a preference for live action and direct involvement in meetings and decision-making settings, but the press of events can impair the quality of decision-taking. Just as fieldworkers have to establish priorities for their limited resource of time, so too must managers order their time to the greatest effect.

Few social work managers apply a behavioural analysis to their own performance. The manager in an industrial concern will be judged by his impact on productivity and profitability. While the quality of management is not the only factor influencing those outcomes, the causal relationship is sufficiently clear for it to lead to the dismissal or demotion of managers who fail. As local government comes under closer public scrutiny, it is timely to look for ways in which objective tests of effectiveness can be applied in the managerial context.

The Code of Practice on Annual Reports, issued after the Local Government (Planning and Land) Act (1980), is a useful starting point. The aim of the government is to increase the volume of information available to ratepayers, to provide uniform measures of performance, and to encourage comparison of the relative cost effectiveness of the individual local authority with its geographical neighbours and with authorities with similar characteristics. In the context of social services, the following indicators have been selected: children in care as a proportion of the population under 18, gross cost per child in care, those over 75 in homes for the elderly as a proportion of the population over 75, gross cost per resident week in homes for the elderly, social work staff per 1000 population, home help contact hours per 1000 population over 65, and net cost of all services per 1000 population.

The choice of indicators is not particularly illuminating, constituting a mixture of financial statistics and service volume statistics with no evident reason for financial statistics being chosen in particular areas rather than in others. The significance of those statistics expressed per 1000 population is that a direct comparison can be made between authorities, a comparison which it is assumed will illuminate the understanding of elected members, officers, and ratepayers and encourage deviant authorities to conform.

It is this last phrase which is crucial. Comparative data is a two-edged sword, for it can be used both to restrain high-spending authorities and to stimulate low-spending authorities. Similar arguments have been used by the local authorities associations in relation to central government's grant-related assessment of what an individual authority should be spending, for it can be used by a socially aware government to punish low-spending authorities as readily as it is being used at present against high spenders. But in the context of social services, it is peculiarly difficult to discern the path of virtue.

Let us consider unit costs of children in residential care. Is it better to have a high unit cost or a low one? A low unit cost may be indicative of a very efficient, cost-conscious administration. It is more likely to indicate poor staffing ratios and little individual attention. Conversely, a high unit cost may indicate profligacy; it is, however, equally likely to be caused by high staffing ratios, or high overtime payments to cover staff absences, or a successful preventive child care policy which has reduced the numbers of children in residential care. And the unit costs invariably reflect far more than the staffing levels prevailing in the home. For instance, the incidence of debt charges will be higher on a new purpose-built home but could be nil on a Victorian converted property; differential levels of expenditure on maintenance will be reflected in unit costs; and the form of heating in use will also affect running costs. It is straining credulity to expect this degree of detailed information to be presented and understood in relation to all inter-authority comparisons, yet without it the whole exercise is unproductive (and certainly not cost effective).

The dangers of inter-authority comparisons (Bamford and East-burn 1980) have been discussed elsewhere but whatever their weaknesses they will be used, misused, and abused as a result of current legislation. Managers need then to be aware of all the qualifications which need to be applied if only to reassure councillors that statistics continue to obey Disraeli's famous dictum. At worst, the financial comparisons could be used as the instrument to apply industrial concepts of productivity. Members might set as a target a 5 per cent reduction in unit costs in residential care. Basically this could be achieved in two ways – by pushing up occupancy levels, possibly accepting persons in residential care who do not need to be there, or by reducing staffing levels. Such a target would, it is evident, be a gross oversimplification of a complex problem, but central government has shown the way with its simplistic approach to local democracy and the example given may not be wholly fanciful.

Even if the worst excesses of oversimplification are avoided, there can be no doubt that the quest for value for money will continue. And it is to this challenge that managers will need to respond. It necessitates a critical re-evaluation of all the work currently undertaken with a financial cost attached to each aspect of social welfare provision. One does not have to adopt the terminology of zero base budgeting to undertake a similar exercise. The issues which are raised in such a re-examination are first the value of provision to individuals and the community, and second the degree to which existing provision may be substitutable – or to put it more crudely but honestly, can jobs now done by highly paid staff be done just as well by lower-paid staff or volunteers?

Measuring effectiveness of provision is difficult. Measuring value is even more so for it raises philosophical and ethical questions. If a domiciliary visiting service of the elderly has no measurable impact in terms of delaying or reducing the need for hospital or Part III care it may sound to be ineffective; if it improves the quality of life of the elderly and brings them comfort, can it be held to be without value? A balance sheet has therefore to recognize that there are elements of social value which are unquantifiable, but nevertheless worthwhile. A comprehensive assessment of a service would need to examine the cost of providing it, the effectiveness of the service in achieving its stated objectives both generally and with individual clients, the benefit to clients of the service, and the impact – financial, social, and resource – of discontinuing the service.

Substitutability is a fashionable concept. It has obvious political attractions especially at a time of restraint on public spending, and has professional advantages too. It can be applied to different client groups. Child care services, and in particular those for the young offender, are being rethought with a reduction of residential provision and priority given to intermediate treatment and community care. These services are both less expensive and more effective. Mentally handicapped persons now in hospital care could be supported in the community through hostels and group homes, again with the dual benefit of financial savings for the local authority and improved quality of life for the individual. And elderly persons, otherwise destined to go into Part III accommodation, could be sustained and supported in the community by improved domiciliary services, and by an extension of the sheltered housing concept. A further area in which substitutability has been discussed is the use of social work assistants on work currently carried out by qualified social workers.

The political enthusiasm for patchwork also carries some overtones of the substitutability concept. If locally based neighbourhood workers, operating either as volunteers or for nominal reward, can be deployed to reduce the workload of professional staff, they create an opportunity for staff savings and consequently a reduced overall level of expenditure. Expressing reservations about the desirability of substitution on this scale is to run the risk of accusations of professional self-interest. The reality, however, is that the practicability of substitutability needs to be considered as part of the critical reassessment of existing services, but that in some situations it would be achieved only at the cost of diluting the quality of care. For instance, a network of parents and volunteers could be used to support families of mentally handicapped children; it will do so most effectively when it is complementary to, rather than a substitute for, local authority services.

Resources

Substitutability is an important issue precisely because there are limited resources, and making optimum use of those resources is a problem facing all managers. To Chief Officers it presents strategic choice of the kind implicit in substitutability; to middle managers it involves the rationing of already limited services and the consistent application of criteria for those services; to first-line managers it poses the issue of maintaining staff morale and high standards when demands for services are not matched by concomitant staffing growth or service provision.

The contraction of physical resources which has imposed these strains on managers is likely to continue. While there may be shifts of emphasis reflecting changes in political control, these are more likely to have an impact on capital investment and transfer payments than on the share of national resources given to personal social services. How then can managers handle the tensions which will inevitably arise? One suggestion made by Hill (1979) following the DHSS study (Parsloe and Stevenson 1978), is that decentralization can do much to ease the tensions and frustrations of social workers which accumulate when decisions about resources (in particular, the allocation of places in residential care) are taken by headquarters staff removed from the daily contact with clients in need. Social workers were far more satisfied with arrangements which led to their close involvement with colleagues allocating resources. In passing, it is an intriguing commentary on the politicization of social workers that Hill found social workers seeing the acquisition of resources for their clients as a head-to-head confrontation with those 'up there' controlling the resources but regarded attempts to influence wider resource allocation decisions as inappropriate.

The study found that social workers both as individuals and as team members were not interested in or optimistic about influencing departmental policy. The limitations on senior managers were imperfectly understood, and the concepts of resource allocation unfamiliar. The distinction between proportional and individual justice is critical to an understanding of the constraints on policy formation, yet is imperfectly appreciated by social workers. Individual or 'creative' justice is concerned with the unique needs of individuals. It is commonly the perspective of social workers, who by virtue of their training and their involvement with clients seek to achieve justice for the individual, family, or group with whom they are working. By contrast, proportional justice describes the concern of the administration to ensure fairness between the competing claims for priority of different clients. It is the need for proportional justice which leads to the fixing of criteria, or priorities, when resources are limited, and to the attempt to secure consistency of treatment. There is an inherent tension between individual and proportional justice. Middle managers have to hold that tension and reflect the wider concerns of senior management to ensure equitable distribution of resources.

Territorial justice is an important variant on the theme of proportional justice, with particular implications for local government services. There is a need to ensure a fair distribution of resources between different areas in a local authority. An area may have spent its full budgetary allowance of Section 1 money and feel aggrieved by the refusal of central management to increase its allocation. To the managers however that area may have received a fair share of available funds, and may be viewed as applying substantially different criteria to the use of Secion 1 money to the detriment of territorial justice.

These issues are rarely considered on social work training courses. Writing of discretion, Parsloe and Stevenson consider the rival claims of proportional and creative justice.

'Social workers have a tendency to assume that the latter must always prevail and this notion may have gone unchallenged during training. In fact, the ethos of many courses probably gives it positive support. Discretion, and responsibility and accountability of which it is part, are important issues for social workers and affect their day to day work with clients and as members of an organis-

ation. Yet we did not get the impression that in basic or in service training they had sufficient opportunities to discuss them.'
(Parsloe and Stevenson 1978: 357)

And again when considering the relationship between professional responsibility and accountability to the organization and to the public, they found that social workers 'were extremely confused and few gave us reason to think they had had opportunities either on their basic course or during in service training to discuss and clarify these issues' (Parsloe and Stevenson 1978: 356).

This is not to argue that the function of training is to turn out a fully equipped local authority social worker. It is however vital that training should afford an adequate preparation for work in the major employment settings. There is abundant evidence from research (Parsloe and Stevenson 1978; Sainsbury 1980) that the importance of the agency setting as an influence on practice has been insufficiently appreciated, and that the result is to fuel the confusion and uncertainty of newly qualified workers returning to an agency.

In other areas, management can look to technological development for assistance to cope with contracting resources. Social work's use of technology hitherto has been hesitant, limited to alarm systems for the elderly. But used properly, computerization could facilitate cumbrous administrative procedures. (Although if print-outs are circulated to all those affected with the cheerful abandon that photocopies are circulated, the piles of computer paper will be huge.) But when it comes to the computerization of client data, there is justifiable concern to ensure that confidentiality is protected adequately. LAMSAC is currently working on a draft code of practice to safeguard clients' rights where social services data is stored in a computer, but however rigorous the safeguards new technology will arouse anxieties. One of these is the threat posed to jobs, and those threatened are not only clerical and administrative. Review visiting of the elderly has already been mentioned critically, but its value would be even more questionable if a central control had aural and visual contact with old people living alone. There is something of a Big Brother flavour to such a concept, but if it serves to protect the old and the frail more effectively than any other method and the client is willing to accept this scrutiny difficulties may be overcome. The use of such technology will however raise both ethical and labour problems different from those with which social work managers have become familiar.

Changes in service provision

The bipartisan approval of voluntarism, exemplified by the launch of the Good Neighbour campaign and the endorsement of patchwork by successive Secretaries of State for Social Services, is likely to continue. It is at once a moral good and an economic necessity, a combination of immense political appeal. But the greater involvement of volunteers, the diversification of fieldwork roles, and the decentralization inherent in the patchwork approach require managers to rethink some of their usual notions of hierarchy and accountability.

BASW's evidence to the Barclay Inquiry into the roles and tools of local authority social workers offers one possible way forward. In its voluminous evidence, BASW asserted that it

'has consistently adopted the stance that the social work function must be explicitly differentiated from the social service function . . . The social service function is largely an administrative or practical occupation, involving the performance of prescribed tasks. The social work function is the creative application of acquired skills based on stated values and designed to help people in need by means of interpersonal relationships between worker and client, who may be an individual, a family, a group or a community.'

(BASW 1981: 30)

This definition is open to challenge, not least in its dismissive treatment of social service functions, but it does stress an important point which is still sometimes overlooked. Social workers constitute a small proportion of the total work-force of social services. While gatekeepers to departmental resources, they see fewer clients than are seen by home helps in the course of the year. Social services departments then are not synonomous with social work.

An earlier BASW paper from the Career Grade Working Party, had developed the argument of a separation between social work and social services functions. It suggested that there should be a radical restructuring of social services department distinguishing between professional practice and administration. It argued that a model to be considered was that of the medical profession in hospitals where the hierarchy is professional. 'The managerial responsibility of the consultant is focused upon enabling junior colleagues to improve their professional practice, not at removing accountability from them . . . An hierarchical structure is not necessarily anti-professional' (BASW 1975: 283). This last point is worth further consideration. What the BASW working party proposed was the substitution of a practice-orientated hierarchy for the managerial hierarchy in social work agencies. Its remedy was rooted in the importance of senior members of the profession remaining in practice, not in any innate hostility to hierarchies.

The emphasis which the BASW report placed on social work breaking free from the shackles of unresponsive and unsympathetic administration has been echoed in the writings of Jordan. He has argued that 'it is the mixture of public assistance and social work that is so fatal to the social workers' professional task' (Jordan 1974: 181) and contends that the association of social services departments with the relieving functions of former welfare departments contributes to a stigmatization of social work clients.

BASW in 1975 argued for a clear division between social work and administration, Jordan for a removal of income maintenance responsibilities from social services departments, and Butrym developed a case that 'a social work department or division within the total social services department structure should be created and run by social workers on professional lines' (Butrym 1976: 145).

This potentially powerful lobby has failed to develop support, and ironically a prime reason is the creation of the Certificate in Social Service. Butrym felt that CSS was 'an important step forward in the establishment of a clearer distinction between social work and social services provision' (Butrym 1976: 138). In practice however CSS has served further to blur the demarcation lines between those with a social work qualification and other workers in social services departments. CSS training is based on close collaboration between the agency and the college, and is a form of 'on the job' training specifically geared to be relevant to the individual work situation. As such, it contrasts sharply with CQSW training which some Directors of Social Services have contended serves to unfit people for practice. The blurring which has taken place has been influenced by two factors. First, CSS has been developed as a qualification in fieldwork, day care, and residential settings alongside CQSW but without a clear delineation of respective roles between CQSW and CSS holders. Second, there has been increasing demand within CSS courses for training in the area of interpersonal relationships. While it is the official policy of the Central Council for Education and Training in Social Work that CSS is not a qualification in social work, in practice a substantial part of many courses is given over to casework and group-work under the heading of 'interpersonal relationships'.

The Birch Report on manpower and training for the social services (Birch Report 1976) envisaged a changing pattern of fieldwork deployment with the growing use of social service officers taking over functions performed by social work assistants, but doing so with the benefit of a CSS training and with a designation which accurately reflected their role. The dramatic growth of CSS envisaged by the Birch Report has not taken place, largely as a result of the changed economic environment, and the majority of those who have taken CSS have come from residential, day care and domiciliary services. Despite this, a number of departments have now acquired experience of dividing tasks between CQSW holders and social service officers. The division works well as long as the junior grade remains unqualified as the more complex work, that involving client vulnerability or involving a change of residence, has clearly to go to qualified staff. But when social service officers become qualified, adding training to long experience, it becomes more difficult to argue that they are less well equipped to assess the need of an elderly client for a Part III place than a newly qualified CQSW holder.

In its evidence to the Barclay Inquiry (BASW 1981), BASW submitted a list of twenty-five tasks and indicated against each the appropriate worker to undertake the task from four staff groups – social workers, occupational therapists, social service officers, and assistants. Deciding on the need for admission to residential care and arranging placement, for example, is designated a social worker's function; organizing occupation and recreation but not as part of an individual rehabilitative or therapeutic programme is designated as a social service officer function: and the physical care of handicapped people is seen as a role for an assistant (a category which appears to embrace both care assistants and home helps). Yet BASW denies the logic of its own division between social service and social work by designating certain functions, for example the provision of welfare rights advice, assessment for and provision of various tangible personal social services, and the recruitment and deployment of volunteer labour as appropriate for either or both social workers and social service officers. The logic of identifying these tasks as those for social service officers is undermined by current practice where social workers are actively involved in these areas. Yet the frontiers of social workers' involvement have to be rolled back if a distinction is to be drawn between social services provision and social work.

If there are problems in effecting this distinction in fieldwork, they become more acute in residential and day care settings. At least in fieldwork settings, some attempt at identifying the task required can be made at the time of referral and the appropriate allocation made. In residential care, all those in the home from the officer in charge to the humblest domestic worker are directly involved in contact and relationships with residents. It is for this reason that the Residential Care Association has argued that it is impossible to differentiate residential work according to social work and social service components.

The changing nature of residential care has led to a blurring of boundaries between field and residential settings. It has led to an extension of the role of the residential worker as the key worker concept has been widely utilized. It has required definition of the objectives of residential care, and focused attention on improving the quality of life in homes. Confronted with these changes, it is interesting to note the basis of distinction proposed by BASW. For workers responsible for other staff and working directly with residents experiencing serious emotional or social difficulties, CQSW is seen as the most suitable training. By contrast, CSS is seen as the qualification for those caring directly for residents and often responsible for a variety of domestic tasks. This distinction has the virtue of neatness. But it does not accord with reality. CQSW holders become involved with domestic tasks in mental handicap, child care, and elderly establishments – and usually other staff become involved with 'residents experiencing serious emotional or social difficulties'. Sometimes it happens by default when senior or qualified staff are unavailable, but more often by the deliberate choice of the resident in whom to confide.

The rigid demarcation of tasks cannot be justified conceptually, whether by reference to the nature of the client group served, the respective training courses, or the needs of individual clients. Both in fieldwork and residential settings what is required is a flexible use of staff, for what has emerged from the preoccupation of the last decade with defining the social work task is that it is a chimera. While one can indeed identify certain tasks for which social work skills are required, there is a large boundary area where a social work qualification is but one of several possible suitable preparations for practice. The advent of CSS has thrown this boundary area into relief, and social work managements have to respond accordingly.

This means using staff flexibly, encouraging CSS holders to develop specialist roles and taking another look at the right balance between qualified and unqualified staff. It means an end to some professional pretensions that social work can be rigidly demarcated in the same way as older professions. The fluidity which is advocated is however wholly in line with the way in which social work has evolved. But creating and using flexible staff roles places demands on management, for the optimum use of resources will only come about if the manager is responsive both to the changing needs of the area and the changing balance within the group of staff as individuals leave or workers develop in confidence and skills.

Alternative structures

The three factors discussed above taken together place heavy burdens on all levels of management. But there is an alternative view, which sees the development of managerial functions as an unnecessary excrescence on the body of social work, which rejects the necessity of hierarchical controls, and which looks for a development of professional autonomy to counteract the pernicious growth of managerial orientation in social work.

A recurrent theme in this book has been the uneasy marriage of social work with the traditions of local government. Yet if a structural solution in the sense of removing social work from the local government context is discounted – notwithstanding occasional DHSS flirtations with linking health care and social services provision – it is necessary to look at ways in which the undeniable tensions within existing structures can be converted from destructive to creative.

The advent of level three workers has led some areas to consider viewing such workers as self-regulating professionals as suggested by the Career Grade Working Party (BASW 1975). Sometimes this is described as professional autonomy although there is a tendency to use the phrase without looking in detail at what it means. The only workers with complete professional autonomy are those in private practice whose accountability is only to the client. The agency setting acts as a constraint on all social workers. Sainsbury's research (Sainsbury 1980) demonstrated that it also influenced practice with workers in different agencies having differing perceptions and priorities. But if autonomy does not mean total freedom of action, what do social workers understand by the term?

LIMITS ON AUTONOMY

It means the individualization of practice with social workers using their judgement in reaching decisions rather than making decisions on the basis of preordained rules and procedures. To that point there are few fetters upon autonomy. While instances still occur where seniors instruct staff to take a child into care, or to make a particular recommendation in a court report, such intervention can be justified only in the most extreme circumstances where the social worker's judgement is palpably unreasonable. As a statement of principle however the views of the worker who has seen the client should be preferred to those of senior staff who have not. The attitude to supervision taken by many senior social workers reflects this approach. But no autonomy can be unrestricted in an agency; three major limiting factors can be identified – professional, political, and resource constraints.

The professional restraint is one which operates through the agency, which incorporates certain values. A probation officer, interviewing a man who has shot and killed a police officer, might conclude that he had serious personal problems which could be helped by probation supervision. Nevertheless such a recommendation would be unacceptable to his managers because it would be wholly unrealistic and likely to bring the agency into disrepute with the judiciary if it was submitted. In similar fashion, a social worker with strong views about child abuse who sought a place of safety order in every instance where a child was injured would rapidly come into conflict with the professional values of the agency for failing to individualize treatment. Agency expectations are then a powerful influence on decision-making.

Political constraints were discussed in Chapter 5. They come into play when elected members seek to influence decisions. The member certainly has a right to enquire into the way in which a particular client is being handled, and the criteria being applied in relation to the offer or withholding of a service. It is appropriate for managers to review the way in which social workers have exercised their discretion if members so request, but as was stated earlier it would be equally appropriate for management to uphold the social worker's exercise of discretion (even if they disagreed with it) providing that it was a reasonable decision. Ultimately the power of decision by statute rests with the Committee. It would be a foolish and arrogant Committee which overruled professional decisions taken reasonably and backed by the Chief Officer. That ultimate authority does however act as a constraint on workers' autonomy, because workers are conscious in their practice that their decision will not be final in every case.

While the constraints of professional values and political intervention are important and sometimes dramatic, for most social workers the limitation on their autonomy of which they are most conscious stems from the lack of resources. Although designated gatekeepers to the treasure chest of social services provision, social workers rarely have the personal authority to spend money directly. There is a rich irony in contemporary practice. Decisions to admit children to care are usually taken by a social worker and his first-line manager. Such decisions have very substantial financial consequences. Yet if a social worker wanted a cash sum equivalent to the cost of keeping that child in care for a week, the decision would be taken at a far more senior level in the hierarchy. Preventive work involving expenditure is thus immediately removed from the autonomous control of the worker.

Many social work decisions have resource implications, for access to services – in particular residential care, but also day care services, intermediate treatment, and some domiciliary services – is often dependent on a full social work assessment. BASW's evidence to the Barclay Inquiry says that

'the social worker should, according to his professional assessment, and taking into account a client's preference and, as appropriate the opinions of other colleagues, identify the range of services which he or she believes would best suit the person in need. Having presented the assessment, and in discussion with managerial staff, decisions will be taken as to whether, in the case of this particular client, there are the available resources which are required. It is a responsibility of management to determine the best use of resource allocation in an area.'   (BASW 1981)

Here then is a clear division between the autonomy of the worker – freedom to make recommendations appropriate to the needs of the client – and the responsibility of managers to allocate resources as they judge appropriate. It sets a limit to autonomy and acts as a real constraint on professional decision-making. There is little point in deciding that a day nursery place is exactly the type of support needed by young parents having difficulty in handling their children if the worker knows that such a resource is already oversubscribed. Similarly, a recommendation for residential care for a frail old person living alone not only has to be approved by the manager controlling that resource, but has to compete with similar recommendations from other fieldworkers.

This discussion illustrates the severe limitations that exist in practice on professional autonomy, limitations that are not the result of oppressive and bureaucratic hierarchies but which exist in the very nature of human need, which cannot be fully matched by available resources.

HIERARCHY OR POLYARCHY

The central task facing social work managers is to effect the combination of maximum decentralization, delegation, and professional autonomy with a strong central planning and policy-making capacity. The latter is vital as long as social services remain within local government. While it would be wholly in tune with the ethos of social work practice to reduce the layers of hierarchy, it should be acknowledged that in a local government context a hierarchy does bring some benefits to the agency. In his relationship with other Chief Officers, the Director's status is important. Salary, span of control, and number of staff all influence that perception. A wholly polyarchic structure would not only be an alien in the local government environment, but would deprive social work of an effective voice in the wider resource-allocation decisions. Hill is quoted above as noting social workers' readiness to ignore these aspects, but such a blinkered view fails to take into account the real knowledge and contribution which social workers can offer in relation to housing, education, planning, and employment issues.

PARTICIPATION AND AUTHORITY

The lack of participation in policy formation is curious given that most departments would affirm their belief in a participatory approach. Unfortunately 'participation', like 'accountability', is a word which generates heat rather than light for it means different things to different people. To management it can mean little more than the opportunity for staff to comment upon policy decisions which have effectively been taken, or to express their views but with no assurance that they will be heeded. Staff consultation/participation in appointments is an example of this semantic confusion.

When staff are offered the opportunity to participate in the appointment of, for example, an Area Officer, that participation can take many forms. It is possible for the staff to elect a representative to sit on the appointing committee. The representative is likely to be outnumbered by management. The participation while direct thus has elements of tokenism. Furthermore, it raises the issue of the appropriateness of a member of staff engaging in the interview and appointment of his future manager. But if the staff representative is not a member of the interviewing panel, how are staff views to be conveyed? Some authorities have used a two-tier structure with a group interview by Area staff and a formal interview by the appointing group. Alternatively, the Area views on applicants can be fed back informally to the appointing panel. Yet in none of the examples cited does management in any way relinquish its right and responsibility to take the ultimate decisions. Problems arise when the exact boundaries of staff participation are not clearly defined in advance by management, leading to a sense of bitterness if the preferred candidate of staff is not appointed.

Participation can only be effective if there is a shared commitment by management and staff with management clearly defining the use it will make of and weight accorded to staff views and staff accepting the responsibility funnelling its views to management. Parsloe and Stevenson suggest that confusion about the nature of authority is a factor impairing staff relationships with management.

Authority is a problem area for social workers. While it is part of the daily bread and butter task for probation officers who have to think through the authority vested in them and how they use it, local authority social workers continue to find difficulty in seeing and using the positive elements in authority. In the training context, this finds expression in the reluctance to fail students – a reluctance well documented and widely acknowledged within social work (M. Davies and Brandon 1979). In fieldwork practice, the reluctance of social workers to use authority to exercise control has led to an upsurge in the numbers committed to Borstal and detention centres. While social workers often blame the magistracy for this latter development the truth is both more prosaic and more alarming. Thorpe *et al.* (in press) have demonstrated that custodial sentences are the result of social work recommendations made when it is felt that control is needed, yet ignoring the potential control that can be exercised in the community setting. This ambivalence about authority also infects some social work managers, who effectively deny the reality of their position by yielding up their decision-making responsibilities to the group or the team. Of course this may sometimes be the best approach providing that the manager is clear that the ultimate responsibility is his even if he chooses in a particular situation to accept the democratic view. Paradoxically, this quasi-democratic approach may make it more difficult for newly qualified workers to accept the limits which are set to participation when vital decisions arise.

Confusions

In reviewing the current state of the art of management in relation to social work, a number of confusions have been identified. It has been suggested that many of the terms most frequently used in discussion of management – supervision, accountability, participation, autonomy – are used more as slogans than as precise definitions. It has further been suggested that the current disarray of social work owes much to its failure to specify clearly what it can and cannot realistically be expected to achieve, and that management must bear the primary responsibility for this failure. The unique nature of social work is heavily relied upon by apologists for social work. A similar argument is used by many social work managers to disclaim the relevance of management training to the special demands of social work management, yet in each of the areas reviewed the need to apply management rather than social work skills has become evident.

But the application of management skills has to be allied to organizational structures which reflect the needs of social work. This means the acceptance of structures which emphasize decentralization of decision-making, define the role of staff participation in policy formation, and differentiate staff roles within a teamwork context. The experiments now taking place on patchwork will only be effective if they succeed in drawing support from the neighbourhood and allowing the needs of the neighbourhood to influence the pattern of provision. Holding the balance between territorial justice and responsiveness to neighbourhood needs is not an easy task. The social work manager in the more open and equal relationship with both clients and staff that is being envisaged will have to rely less on the authority invested by status within the agency and far more on personal qualities of leadership to achieve results.

The corollary of the growth of consumer and community influence is the weakening of the rigidities of line management structures. At the same time, the role of the first-line manager is under challenge from the growing numbers of experienced and qualified workers seeking recognition and responsibility and hence unwilling to accept a directive, controlling relationship with their manager. No dramatic changes will come about swiftly, for the trends identified are long-term shifts of attitude. By the end of the decade however one can anticipate a far slimmer management structure than currently exists, with, in particular, substantial reductions at senior social worker level, and a pattern of service delivery which places formal responsibility on individual practitioners. It will not constitute the professional autonomy of the hospital consultant, but few social workers would wish to emulate that model where accountability is subjugated to clinical freedom. The more likely model for social work is one of clearly defined professional responsibility but where formal accountability is not solely discharged through line management but takes full account of consumer, neighbourhood, and fellow professional influences, possibly through the local committee suggested by Sainsbury considered in Chapter 7 (Sainsbury 1981).

Conclusion

Social work is peculiarly vulnerable to the Peter Principle whereby people are promoted to the level beyond their competence. The criteria for promotion to first-line managerial posts are undefined with the result that capable practitioners are selected for their social work ability rather than their managerial skills. While this has been criticized for denuding social work of its base of skilled practitioners, it is equally pertinent to note that it leaves social work with poorly motivated and ill-equipped managers.

There can be no prescription for the ideal social work manager. Some of the skills needed have been discussed in this book, but no manager can be expected to be proficient in all of them. Indeed at different levels of management, the emphasis will shift. While the preoccupation of the first-line manager will be with staff supervision, the roles of planner, disturbance handler, negotiator, and figurehead assume greater importance at senior levels of management. But the two basic requirements of a good manager in a social work context are exactly those required of a good manager in any setting, and exactly those embodied in the concept of the managerial grid – concern for people and concern for performance.

Concern for people should be axiomatic in social work. That it is not is a sorry reflection of the depersonalization of hierarchical institutional structures, and of the insecurity of some managers which is expressed in what I earlier described as a 'macho' attitude of using their authority to force through policies with no scope for flexibility or compromise. Yet that aspect needs to be at the core of managerial practice. It involves concern for clients and the service they receive. How quickly is the phone answered? Are letters responded to promptly? Is the reception area comfortable and welcoming? Is a client being scapegoated by the office? These are the kind of questions that the manager has to ask about overall procedures and policies as well as about the quality of individual work. But concern for clients is only one half of the people-orientation required of the manager, for concern has also to be shown for staff. This involves a fair distribution of work, the capacity to recognize when a worker is under pressure, and to offer relief, the creation of harmonious and flexible working relationships, the ready transmission of information, and a genuine interest in the well-being of staff. It is extraordinary how insensitive social workers can be to the needs of clerical and administrative staff, but with the spread of the team approach there is a growing recognition of the contribution of non-professionals.

The other pole in the managerial grid is that of concern for performance. Throughout the book I have argued that managers need to be highly specific about their objectives, need to define these in behavioural and measurable terms wherever possible, and need to respond positively to the calls for greater effectiveness and demonstrations of the cost benefit of social work intervention. It is in these ways that the fuzziness of many managerial concepts can be pared down to their essential elements and by a combination of the people and performance orientations, the 9:9 manager of the managerial grid can be achieved who is able to reconcile systematic, goal-setting, decisive leadership with the human insights of social work.

Achieving this combination will not be easy. It will require a higher level of investment in management training, an intellectual discipline foreign to contemporary social work practice, and a strong professional leadership. Without it, however, social work clients will continue to receive a less effective service than they need and than they are entitled to expect a decade after social services reorganization.

Postscript: The Barclay Report

Shortly before this book went to press, the report of the Barclay Committee (Barclay Report 1982) was published. The Committee had been charged by the then Secretary of State for Social Services with the task of inquiring into the role and tasks of social workers. Its work took fifteen months, and constitutes a major statement about the current constraints and future direction of social work. Many of the issues considered in the Report echo points discussed earlier in this book, and the recommendations have considerable implications for the style and responsibility of social work management.

The Report saw social workers as having two areas of responsibility. First, they have a continuing responsibility for social casework – the counselling of individuals and families with difficulties. Second, they have a responsibility for what the Committee termed social care planning – the development of strategies to provide effective community support including community development and the necessary social and political action. Throughout the Report, there was a strong emphasis on the decentralization of power and authority to enable social workers fully to utilize existing networks in the community, and on the need for a working partnership between social workers, clients, and the community. The development of patchwork was seen as a significant element in the process of bringing social workers closer to the communities which they serve.

Patchwork however was not seen by the Committee as the only means whereby a greater community orientation can be promoted.

The development of residential establishments as resource centres for the local communities in which they are situated was endorsed in the Report as was the imaginative use of outposting to locate social workers in the settings from which work would be derived. Managers were urged to encourage the greatest possible delegation of decision making to social workers and their immediate managers and to make the policy-making machinery less remote. The Report accepted that the relaxation of rigid controls carried certain risks, but felt that these were necessary if the practice of social work was not to be inhibited.

The stance of the Report was strongly in favour of the formalization of clients' rights through appeals and grievance procedures. Extending protection to clients through the creation of an independent inspectorate was viewed sympathetically by the Committee although the machinery by which inspection could best be facilitated was not fully worked out.

Four key issues discussed in the book are considered in some detail in the Report. These are issues of accountability (Chapter 3, pp. 24–8), teamwork and the development of a community approach (Chapters 5 and 6, pp. 71–89 and 95–9), planning and participation (Chapter 7, pp. 113–37), and organizational structures and their impact on practice (Chapters 6 and 9, pp. 90–112 and 166–75). Each has significant implications for social work managers, who have an important role in deciding whether or not to implement the recommendations in the Report – most of which are addressed to agency managers rather than local authorities or central Government.

Accountability

In discussing accountability, six different but related forms of accountability were identified in Chapter 3. To these, the Report adds a seventh, suggesting that in addition to social workers' accountability to clients there is also accountability to the informal carers and support networks with whom social workers are involved. Now multiple accountability is an inescapable part of the responsibilities carried by social workers, but the task of managers is to clarify and make explicit who is accountable to whom for which aspect of work. The Report appears to be confusing differing forms of accountability. There can be little doubt that social workers have obligations in respect of informal carers. They include the provision of relevant information, the offer of support, and participation in planning for the needs of clients. But these obligations are different from accountability, with its implication of formalized relationships. In clarifying accountability for staff, managers are therefore likely to rely on more limited definitions. Disentangling the nature of accountability for employers and clients respectively is extremely complex when the demands of the two are in conflict. Despite the rhetoric of partnership in the Report, the formal accountability of social workers to their employers is likely to preclude general acceptance of the concept that they are also formally accountable to informal carers.

Some of the mechanisms suggested in the Report for strengthening the rights of clients also raise the issue of political accountability considered in Chapter 6 (pp. 135–36). Reference was made there to the problem which the concept of shared care can present to traditional patterns of accountability to employers. By developing informal community resources, the degree of direct control which management can exercise is reduced. Sainsbury's suggestion of a modified version of a probation case committee (Chapter 6, p. 111) was picked up by the Report, which terms such a body a local welfare advisory committee. This would serve as a forum for clients, employers, and social workers to discuss agency policies which impinge on the rights of clients including confidentiality, access to information, and resource allocation, as well as monitoring the implementation of appeals procedures.

How far will employing agencies be willing to go in ceding power over these areas? The sensitivity of press and public to cases where clients appear to be denied access to their own files, as in the Gaskin case in Liverpool, or where clients are the subject of remote decisions without having the opportunity to be heard, constitutes a clear indication of the difficulties which might lie ahead. On agency policy the employing body has to remain the final arbiter, but if issues of policy are considered by the local welfare advisory committee, which comes to a different view, the potential for conflict is great.

Where there are questions about the competence or judgement of individual social workers, the Report states that the initial and primary responsibility must rest with senior management. An independent second opinion was suggested as the means whereby clients' rights can be protected. While emphasis placed on protecting the interests of clients in the unequal power relationship between them and social workers is welcome, it poses potential problems for managers. First, they have to continue the efficient dispatch of the agency's workload while ensuring full explanations are given to clients, decisions are notified in writing, appeals and complaints procedures are properly operated, and second opinions are sought. Second, they have to support individual members of staff whose judgement is overturned by a second opinion, and help them to accept this constructively. Third, they must strive to avoid actions which might generate complaints from clients. The Report recognizes that social workers, their managers, and employing agencies will be more vulnerable than at present with an increase in clients' rights. That vulnerability can only be coped with successfully if managers wholeheartedly accept a commitment to change, while realistically recognizing the problems which this will present. Holding this balance will require skills in negotiation and advocacy as well as the more traditional supervisory skills.

Teamwork and the community approach

Three types of social work teams were considered in Chapter 5 – traditional, transitional, and community teams (pp. 71–4). The Report puts its weight wholeheartedly behind the community team model in which 'social workers are involved in a network which can be described as part of the community support system'. Community social work is not presented in the Report as a blueprint, but rather as an attitude of mind.

Some of the skills required of managers in developing a community approach are identified in the Report. They include entrepreneurial skills in bargaining over resources for teams and community groups, negotiating skills in linking with voluntary organizations and self-help groups, and planning skills to ensure that the views of the team and the surrounding community are taken into account in agency planning. The discussion in Chapter 6 of the way in which Currie and Parrott promoted the introduction of a patchwork approach, using the existing resources and strengths of the local community, offers a practical illustration of how these skills can be deployed.

In some ways the Barclay Report appears to go further than Currie and Parrott by suggesting that in some circumstances informal carers and communities should be able to determine how resources are used. This proposition raises again the question of political accountability considered above, but also poses the issue of managerial responsibilities. Managers have a responsibility to ensure that disadvantaged clients – the difficult, dangerous, and dirty – receive a fair allocation of agency resources, although these groups of clients lack informal networks of carers lobbying on their behalf. They have too a responsibility to ensure territorial justice as discussed in the concluding chapter. They will need therefore the strength to resist considerable pressure if they are to achieve fairness in the allocation of resources. Clarity about the degree to which community groups can influence these decisions is therefore particularly important if unrealistic expectations are not to be created.

The shift in emphasis indicated for residential establishments will place new demands on management. Staff will require retraining if they are to add to their existing skills the ability to work positively with community groups. The fortress mentality which characterizes some establishments does give a form of security to staff. Opening up an establishment to outside influences, redefining the role of relatives, friends, and volunteers, and giving more responsibility to residents to organize their own activities removes that security, and lessens the control which staff can exercise. Managers have to help staff to acquire the confidence to take the risks inherent in a more open environment. They have, too, to help them first to identify and second to use the networks which exist within establishments, and which offer links to the wider community.

Planning and participation

The planning responsibility of managers was considered in Chapter 7. It was there suggested that the complex networks with which social work agencies are involved require skills in strategic planning, financial control, and in programming. The Barclay Report gave a strong emphasis to the agency role in social care planning, seeing the development of this approach to social needs as a central element in social work practice.

By social care planning, the Report means the creation with individual clients of a system or network of care, tailored to their particular situation, the integration of potential self-help groups, volunteers, and community organizations into the network, and the identification of general policy issues which affect the client group as a whole. This coherent planning is the exception rather than the norm in current practice It demands different skills from practitioners and managers if it is to be fully implemented.

The knowledge base of managers has to include knowledge of the local community, its key figures, and its important organizations. They can then guide and assist practitioners in their work of developing networks of care. But knowledge of the community can be utilized only if it is accompanied by sensitivity to community needs, and a readiness to listen and to allow community groups to work out their own solutions to problems.

The same issue is present for management as in consideration of teamwork and the community approach. The element of sharing with the community cannot be limited to a sharing of responsibility for those in need, but must include too a sharing of power. Yet, as the Barclay Report points out, the time-scale for change in social care planning is very different from that for the traditional counselling role. The benefits of developing networks of care are both less visible and less immediate. If equal priority is to be given to this aspect of work as to the work of dealing with an individual referral, managers will have to rethink some of their current approaches to allocation and workload measurement, and acknowledge the validity of this indirect work.

The discussion of consumer participation contained in Chapter 7 (pp. 135–37) suggested that the demand for citizen participation had fallen away since the high water mark of 1968. The Barclay Report argued that the trend throughout the 1970s has been towards smaller units of local administration, greater accountability of public agencies, and the reassertion of neighbourhood control, and went on to develop a model of public participation in community social work which goes beyond the tentative prescriptions of the Seebohm Report. The team leader is the pivotal figure in social care planning, receiving all the flow of information from team members about social needs, having a primary role in liaising with community groups, and having the responsibility to influence senior management policies. The skills required, and the organizational structure necessary, to facilitate those responsibilities are the subject of the next section.

Organization and structure

Chapter 6 contended that the organizational structure of social work was changing as a response to new approaches to social work practice, and as a reaction against the rigidities of bureaucratic hierarchies. For managers it was suggested that their role would increasingly be to help social workers relate their work with individuals to the needs of the wider community, that they had to draw on a wide range of interests and experiences to realize the full potential of the team, and that they had to develop new methods to involve local citizens in the structure of provision to create truly community-based services.

The proliferation of tiers of management causes delay in reaching decisions. It causes frustration for frontline workers, and it means that the key decisions are sometimes taken by those who have no personal knowledge of the client. In Chapter 4 (pp. 60–1), it was suggested that the worker with personal knowledge of clients and their needs will usually make a more accurate judgement than can the supervisor acting at one remove. That approach was expressly endorsed by the Report, which argued that decisions about individual clients should not normally be referred above team leader level. The greatest possible degree of formal delegation to frontline social workers and their immediate managers was advocated.

It is important to look at the consequences of implementing delegation and decentralization. First, it removes full control over resource allocation from central management. Second, it can lead to marked differences in practice and level of provision. Third, it runs against the tide of events in social services departments which has pushed important decisions up to senior managers. Fourth, it may leave managers in the unenviable position of having responsibility without power.

The years of cuts have seen a progressive tightening of managerial controls. Decisions with impact on resources – like admission to Part III – are now frequently taken by senior managers, not by social workers. The limitations on resources have forced definition of policy, and the explicit setting down of policies which were formerly ill-defined or undefined. The search for value for money has brought about redeployment from residential to community-based solutions. The inability of departments to pay for expensive placements in community homes has given a far greater impetus to intermediate treatment and domiciliary assessment than have the recommendations of social workers. But all this has been achieved, and the scale of the achievement is often overlooked, through strong central management.

It is important therefore that a strong planning and policy-making capacity should be retained centrally to meet the first two problems set out above. Only thus can the issues of equitable resource allocation between client groups, voluntary organizations, and geographical areas be resolved. But that capacity does not necessitate the same degree of control over operational functions of the agency. Embarking upon the progressive relinquishment of control demands considerable managerial self-confidence. It requires a commitment to ideas of delegation, and a readiness on occasion to accept risks. But it is necessary if agencies are to become more open to influences from the community, and more creative in their approach.

Some of the difficulties posed for management have been identified. The skills required to exercise responsibility by influence rather than control, by natural authority rather than formal status, can meet the third and fourth problems listed above. They can be learned. Indeed they already are, for they are the skills at the core of social work practice based on a value system asserting the rights of individuals, groups, and communities to take decisions for themselves. The social work role may change for managers with perhaps more emphasis on negotiating, planning, and advocacy, and less on counselling. But that management is a social work task was the clear message of the Barclay Report, and of this book.

References

Algie, J. (1975) Social Values, Objectives and Action. London: Kogan Page.

Algie, J. and Miller, C. (1976) Deciding Social Services Priorities. *Social Work Today*, 5 and 19 February.

Algie, J., Hey, A., and Mallen, G. (1981) Cuts – Getting Your Priorities Right. *Community Care*, 6 August.

Allen, D. (1977) The Residential Task – Is There One? *Social Work Today*, 11 October.

Anderson, D. (1979) Enabling Practitioners to Contribute to Practice. *Social Work Today*, 12 June.

Auckland Report (1975) *Report of the Committee of Inquiry into the Provision and Coordination of Services to the Family of J. G. Auckland.* London: HMSO.

Bains Report (1972) *The New Local Authorities Management and Structure.* London: HMSO.

Bamford, T. (1976) Priorities in the Social Services. *Social Work Today* **7** (5).

—— (1978) The Gulf between Managers and Practitioners. *Social Work Today* **10** (10).

Bamford, T. and Eastburn, I. (1980) The Confusion of Making Comparisons. *Municipal Journal*, 5 September.

Banks, G. (1979) Programme Budgeting in the DHSS. In T. Booth (ed.) *Planning for Welfare.* Oxford: Blackwell and Robertson.

Barclay Report (1982) *Social Workers: Their Role and Tasks*. London: Bedford Square Press.

Beveridge Report (1942) *Report on Social Insurance and the Allied Services*. Cmnd. 6404. London: HMSO.

Billis, D., Bromley, G., Hey, A., and Rowbottom, R. (1980) *Organising Social Services Departments*. London: Heinemann.

Bion, W. (1961) *Experiences in Groups*. London: Tavistock.

Birch Report (1976) *Working Party on Manpower and Training for the Social Services*. London: DHSS.

Blake, R. and Mouton, J. (1964) *The Managerial Grid*. Houston: Gulf.

Booth, T. (1979) *Planning for Welfare*. Oxford: Blackwell and Robertson.

Bottoms, A. and McWilliams, W. (1979) A Non-Treatment Paradigm for Probation Practice. *British Journal of Social Work* **9** (2).

Brenton, M. (1978) Worker Participation and the Social Service Agency. *British Journal of Social Work* **8** (3).

Brewer, C. and Lait, J. (1980) *Can Social Work Survive?* London: Temple Smith.

Brill, N. I. (1976) *Teamwork: Working Together in the Human Services*. Philadelphia: Lippincott.

BASW (1975) Report of the Working Party of the British Association of Social Workers on Career Grade. *Social Work Today*, 24 July.

—— (1977) *The Social Work Task*. Birmingham: BASW.

—— (1980a) *Clients Are Fellow Citizens*. Birmingham: BASW.

—— (1980b) *Accreditation in Social Work. Second Report of Joint Steering Group on Accreditation*. Birmingham: BASW.

—— (1981) *Submission to the NISW Working Party on the Role and Tasks of Social Workers*. Birmingham: BASW.

—— (1982) *Report of Project Group on Alternative Structures*. Birmingham: BASW.

Brown Report (1980) *Report of the Committee of Inquiry into the Case of Paul Steven Brown*. Cmnd. 8107. London: HMSO.

Brunel University Institute of Organisation and Social Studies (1974) *Social Services Departments – Developing Patterns of Work and Organisation*. London.

Buckle, J. (1981) *Intake Teams*. London: Tavistock.

Butrym, Z. (1976) *The Nature of Social Work*. London: Macmillan.

Butterworth Inquiry (1972) *Report of the Butterworth Inquiry into the Work and Role of Probation Officers and Social Workers*. Cmnd. 5076. London: HMSO.

Central Council for Educational and Training in Social Work (1974) *People with Handicaps Need Better Trained Workers*. London: CCETSW.

Clarke Report (1979) *Report of the Committee of Inquiry into the Actions of the Authorities and Agencies Relating to Darryn Jones Clarke*. Cmnd. 7730. London: HMSO.

Colwell Report (1974) *Report of the Committee of Inquiry into the Care and Supervision Provided in Relation to Maria Colwell*. London: HMSO.

Currie, R. and Parrott, B. (1981) *A Unitary Approach to Social Work: Application in Practice*. Birmingham: BASW.

Davies, B. (1981) Strategic Goals and Piecemeal Innovations. In E. Goldberg and S. Hatch (eds) *A New Look at the Personal Social Services*. London: Policy Studies Institute.

Davies, B. and Knapp, M. (1978) Hotel and Dependency Costs of Residents in Old People's Homes. *Journal of Social Policy* **7** (1).

Davies, M. and Brandon, J. (1979) The Limits of Competence in Social Work. *British Journal of Social Work* **9** (3).

DHSS (1974) Circular LA (74) (36). *Rate Fund Expenditure and Rate Calls in 75/76*. London: HMSO.

—— (1976) *Priorities for Health and Personal Social Services in England*. London: HMSO.

—— (1977) *The Way Forward*. London: HMSO.

—— (1980) *Reply by the Government to the Third Report from the Social Services Committee 1979–80*. Cmnd. 8086. London: HMSO.

—— (1981a) *Care in Action*. London: HMSO.

—— (1981b) *Care in the Community*. London: HMSO.

—— (1981c) *Staff of Local Authority Social Service Departments at 30.9.80*. S/F81/1. London: DHSS.

Drucker, P. F. (1955) *Practice of Management*. London: Heinemann.

Evans, R. (1978) Unitary Models of Practice and the Social Work Team. In M. R. Olsen (ed.) *The Unitary Model*. Birmingham: BASW.

Fayol, H. (1916) *General and Industrial Management*. London: Pitman.

Ferlie, E. and Judge, K. (1981) Retrenchment and Rationality in the Personal Social Services. *Policy and Politics* **9** (3).

Fischer, J. (1976) *The Effectiveness of Social Casework*. Springfield, Illinois: Charles C. Thomas.

—— (1981) Review in *International Journal of Behavioural Social Work and Abstracts* **1** (1).

Folkard, M. S. (1975) *IMPACT* vol. 1. Home Office Research Study No. 24. London: HMSO.

—— (1976) *IMPACT* vol. 2. Home Office Research Study No. 36. London, HMSO.

Giller, H. and Morris, A. (1981) *Care and Discretion*, London: Burnett Books.

Glastonbury, B. (1975) Cannon Fodder in an Age of Administration. *Social Work Today*, 21 August.

Goffman, E. (1968) *Asylums*. London: Pelican Books.

Goldberg, E. (1978a) *All Things to All Men*. London: National Institute for Social Work.

—— (1978b) Towards Accountability in Social Work: Long Term Social Work in an Area Office. *British Journal of Social Work* **8** (3).

Goldberg, E. and Warburton, W. (1979) *Ends and Means in Social Work*. National Institute of Social Services Library No. 35. London: Allen and Unwin.

Gorham, W. (1967) PPBS – Its Scope and Limits – Notes of a Practitioner. *Public Interest* **8**.

Hadley, R. and McGrath, M. (1980) *Going Local: Neighbourhood Social Services*. London: Bedford Square Press.

Hall, A. (1975) Operational Priority System. *Community Care*, 6 August.

Halmos, P. (1965) *The Faith of the Counsellors*. London: Constable.

Haxby, D. (1978) *Probation – A Changing Service*. London: Constable.

Hey, A. (1982) Third Time Lucky. *Community Care*, 14 January.

Hill, M. and Laing, P. (1979) *Social Work and Money*. London: Allen and Unwin.

Home Office (1965) *The Child, The Family and The Young Offender*. London: Home Office.

Howard, A. and Briers, J. (1979) *An Investigation into the Effect on Clients of Industrial Action by Social Workers in the London Borough of Tower Hamlets.* London: DHSS.

Hudson B. (1975) An Inadequate Personality: A Case Study with a Dynamic Beginning and a Behavioural Ending. *Social Work Today* **6** (16).

—— Behavioural Social Work with Schizophrenic Patients in the Community. *British Journal of Social Work* **8** (2).

Ingleby Report (1960). *Report of the Committee on Children and Young Persons.* London: HMSO.

Jay Report (1979) *Report of the Committee of Enquiry into Mental Handicap Nursing and Care.* Cmnd. 7468. London; HMSO.

Jordan, W. (1974) *Poor Parents.* London: Routledge and Kegan Paul.

Kelly, J. (1974) *Organisational Behaviour.* Homewood, Illinois: Richard D. Irwin.

Kilbrandon Report (1964) *Report of the Committee on Children and Young Persons (Scotland).* Cmnd. 2306. Edinburgh: HMSO.

Longford, Lord (1964) *Crime – A Challenge to Us All.* Report of Labour Party Study Group. London: The Labour Party.

Mcauley P. (1981) Teaching Behaviour Therapy Skills to Social Work Students. *British Journal of Social Work* **11** (2).

Mcauley, R. and Mcauley, P. (1980) The Effectiveness of Behaviour Modification with Families. *British Journal of Social Work* **10** (1).

Mallaby Report (1967) *The Staffing of Local Government.* London: HMSO.

Martinson, R. (1974) What Works – Questions and Answers about Penal Reform. *Public Interest*, spring.

Maud Report (1969) *Report of the Royal Commission on Local Government in England.* Cmnd. 4039. London: HMSO.

Menheniott Report (1978) *Report of the Social Work Service of the DHSS into Certain Aspects of the Management of the Case of Stephen Menheniott.* London: HMSO.

Meurs Report (1975) *Report of the Review Body Appointed to Enquire into the case of Stephen Meurs.* Norwich: Norfolk County Council.

Mintzberg, H. (1973) *The Nature of Managerial Work*. New York: Harper and Row.

Neill, J., Fruin, D., Goldberg, E., and Warburton, W. (1973) Reactions to Integration. *Social Work Today* **4** (15).
Nodder Report (1979) *Organisation and Management of Mental Illness Hospitals*. London: DHSS, HMSO.

Page, R. and Clark, G. A. (eds) (1977) *Who Cares? Young People in Care Speak Out*. London: National Children's Bureau.
Parsloe, P. and Stevenson, O. (1978) *Social Service Teams: The Practitioners' View*. London: HMSO.
Payne, M. (1979) *Power, Authority and Responsibility in Social Services*. London: Macmillan.
Pettes, D. (1979). *Staff and Student Supervision*. London: Allen and Unwin.
Phillips, L. (1980) *Introduction to Decision Analysis*. London: Brunel University Institute of Organisation and Social Studies.

Reid, W. and Epstein, L. (1972) *Task-Centred Casework*. New York: Columbia University Press.
Reid, W. and Shyne, A. (1969) *Brief and Extended Casework*. New York: Columbia University Press.
Report of the Departmental Committee on Social Services in Courts of Summary Jurisdiction (1936). Cmnd. 5122. London: HMSO.

Sainsbury, E. (1980) A Professional Skills Approach to Specialisation. In T. Booth, D. Martin, and C. Melotte (eds) *Specialisation*. Birmingham: BASW/Social Services Research Group.
—— (1981) *Sharing in Welfare: Community Resources and the Work of Area Teams*, Social Work Service No. 27, September. London: HMSO.
Seebohm Report (1968) *Report of the Committee on Local Authority and Allied Personal Social Services*. Cmnd. 3703. London: HMSO.
Shearer, A. (1978) *A Community Service for Mentally Handicapped Children*. London: Dr Barnardo's.
Sheldon, B. (1978) Theory and Practice in Social Work. *British Journal of Social Work* **8** (1).
—— (1982) Review in *British Journal of Social Work* **12** (1).
Simpkin, M. (1979) *Trapped Within Welfare*. London: Macmillan.

Streatfield, D. and Wilson, T. (1980). *The Vital Link: Information in Social Services Departments*. Sheffield: Joint Unit for Social Services Research.

Thorpe, D., Tutt, N., Smith, D., and Green, C. (in press) *Social Work with Juvenile Offenders*. London: Macmillan.

Vickery, A. (1977) *Caseload Management*. National Institute for Social Work Paper No 5. London: NISW.

Webb, A. (1979) Policy Making in Social Services Departments. In T. A. Booth (ed.) *Planning for Welfare*. Oxford: Blackwell and Robertson.

Westheimer, I. (1977) *The Practice of Supervision in Social Work*. London: Wardlock Educational.

Whitmore, R. and Fuller, R. (1980) Priority Planning in an Area Social Services Team. *British Journal of Social Work* **10** (3).

Wilkes, R. (1981) *Social Work with Undervalued Groups*. London: Tavistock Publications.

Younghusband, Dame E. *Social Work in Britain 1950–1975*. London: Allen and Unwin.

Name Index

Subject Index